The Black Arch

HELL BENT

By Alyssa Franke

Published August 2018 by Obverse Books

Cover Design © Cody Schell

Text © Alyssa Franke, 2018

Range Editors: James Cooray Smith, Philip Purser-Hallard

Alyssa would like to thank:

Her family and friends for their support, and her readers for their encouragement and feedback. And a special thank you to Rachel Talalay for providing her visual references and for always being willing to discuss her work with me.

Also Available

For my dad and grandpa, whose memories live on in stories and songs.

And for my mom and grandma, who taught me to be brave.

CONTENTS

OVERVIEW

Serial Title: *Hell Bent*

Writer: Steven Moffat

Director: Rachel Talalay

Original UK Transmission Date: 5 December 2015

Running Time: 1h 00m 29s

UK Viewing Figures: 6.2 million

Regular Cast: Peter Capaldi (The Doctor), Jenna Coleman (Clara)

Recurring Cast: Ken Bones (The General), Maisie Williams (Ashildr), Clare Higgins (Ohila)

Guest Cast: The President (Donald Sumpter), T'nia Miller (Female General), Malachi Kirby (Gastron), Linda Broughton (The Woman), Martin T Sherman (Man), Jami Reid-Quarrell, Nick Ash, Ross Mullen (Wraiths), Nicholas Briggs (Voice of the Dalek)

Antagonists: The Time Lords

Responses:

'There's still poignancy to this goodbye [...] but Clara's is a much more satisfying ending for those who enjoy seeing companions empowered by their time in the TARDIS. It's also relatively fresh ground for **Doctor Who** which often coasts on the fact that the Doctor is omniscient. [...] We need to see the cracks in our heroes from time to time.'

[Joanna Robinson, *Vanity Fair*]

'The latest finale from head writer Steven Moffat feeds heavily on

Doctor Who's rich history, but also draws inspiration from other, more unexpected sources. The end result is mixed, but ultimately this is an episode – and a series – that doesn't quite stick the landing.'

[Morgan Jeffery, *Digital Spy*]

SYNOPSIS

(**Clara** is dead, killed by a Quantum Shade in 21st-century London. **The Doctor** has been betrayed by the Shade's master, the immortal **Ashildr** [1]. After billions of years spent escaping a personalised interrogation device, the Doctor has found himself on Gallifrey for the first time since the Time War [2].)

The furious Doctor returns to the 'Drylands' where he lived as a child (where a **woman** he recognises is concerned for him). He stays there while he plays a waiting game with the Time Lords. They come in turn to invite him to the Capitol – the soldier **Gastron**, to whom the Doctor is a war hero; his superior the **General**; members of the High Council; and finally Lord President **Rassilon** – but he refuses unless Rassilon is exiled for his part in the Time War. After an attempt to have the Doctor executed prompts a military coup in the latter's favour, Rassilon is forced to leave the planet.

The General and **Ohila** of the Sisterhood of Karn plead with the Doctor for information about the **Hybrid** prophesied to destroy Gallifrey. The Doctor insists that if he is to help them Clara must be extracted from her timeline at the moment before her death. As her death is a fixed point, the safety of the universe demands that this should be a strictly temporary measure; however, after asking to borrow a 'human-compatible' neural block, the Doctor takes her and flees. In the process he shoots the General, who obstructs him trying to preserve the timeline, and who regenerates into a new woman.

The Doctor and Clara reach the cloisters beneath the Capitol, where

---

[1] *Face the Raven* (2015).
[2] *Heaven Sent* (2015).

the Matrix is guarded by the cybernetic **Wraiths** of dead Time Lords, and alien intruders imprisoned by the security systems plead for the mercy of death. Clara learns of the Doctor's recent torment, then distracts their pursuers while he arranges their escape. Ohila scolds the Doctor for offering false hope of life to Clara – who indeed is no longer exactly alive. Clara and the Doctor leave in a stolen TARDIS.

However, this does not, as the Doctor hoped, restore Clara to full life. They travel to the very end of the universe, where Ashildr is waiting for them in the ruins of Gallifrey. The Doctor believes Ashildr is the Hybrid, but her theory is that the prophecy refers to the Doctor as he is now, tearing history apart in order to save Clara: she thinks that **Missy** introduced Clara to the Doctor in order to create such a Hybrid. Ashildr joins them in the stolen TARDIS, where the Doctor tries to persuade Clara to accept a memory wipe which will prevent the Time Lords tracking her down. Clara protests, and suggests that erasing the Doctor's memories of her will have the same effect. She believes, but is not certain, that she has reversed the neural block to achieve this. They make their farewells, and activate the device.

In a diner in the Nevada desert, the Doctor has been telling this story – which he has forgotten, but can deduce from the shape its absence leaves in his memory – to the woman behind the counter. In fact she is Clara, and she remembers the Doctor perfectly.

Clara leaves, intent on having new adventures with Ashildr before her final surrender to the Time Lords and to death. The diner – actually the stolen TARDIS – disappears, leaving the Doctor next to his own TARDIS, which still bears **Rigsy**'s graffiti memorial to Clara. It flakes away as the TARDIS dematerialises.

INTRODUCTION

When I first watched the series 9 finale of **Doctor Who**, *Hell Bent* (2015), I was so amazed and excited that I could barely contain myself. I ranted excitedly to my watch party, I sent all-caps tweets to anyone who might care, and I accidentally earned my friend her first noise complaint in her apartment. It is still my favourite finale episode of the series, and one of my favourite companion departure stories ever.

One of the first coherent reactions I tweeted to *Hell Bent* was: 'This is the most explicitly feminist episode of Doctor Who I have ever seen.'[3] For the most part, I stand by that assessment.

Describing an episode as 'feminist' is tricky. There is no singular definition of feminism. There isn't a series of checklists that every feminist has signed off on in order for a work of pop culture to be considered feminist. Feminism is a conflicted space, with frequent (and necessary) discussion and disagreement.

Other feminists would evaluate the relative quality and success of *Hell Bent* differently than I would. But I think it would still be fair to describe *Hell Bent* as a 'feminist' episode because of how deliberately it raises questions about power, privilege, and patriarchy.

Hell Bent questions **Doctor Who**'s recent legacy with companion departures in a way that I have not seen the show do before. It challenges some of the Doctor's most paternalistic, controlling behaviours. Clara Oswald departs with an origin story equal to the Doctor's. And with a Time Lord's on-screen regeneration from a

---

[3] Franke, Alyssa, tweet posted 3:25am GMT, 6 December 2015.

white man into a black woman, the path to Jodie Whittaker's casting as the Doctor (and – hopefully – the casting of a person of colour as the Doctor in the future) became even clearer.

Of course, those aren't the only themes worth exploring in *Hell Bent*. This story shares many narrative similarities with western films, drawing deliberate parallels to one of the great classics, *Shane* (1953). Those western themes are visually reflected by director Rachel Talalay, who was inspired by the visuals of legendary director Sergio Leone. Murray Gold's compositions are gorgeously transformed by Peter Capaldi on the guitar to reflect the 12th Doctor's confusion and grief.

There are smaller touches here, too, which delight. The Sisterhood of Karn returns for the ribbing of Rassilon. We see a TARDIS almost identical to the one flown by the first Doctor. The reappearance of this classic TARDIS is accompanied by possibly the greatest and most meta line in a script ever: 'The Doctor is flying around the classic console, like a distinguished Scottish actor who's slightly too excited for his own good.'[4]

But in my mind, what elevates *Hell Bent* from a good episode to a truly great story is how it isn't afraid to confront **Doctor Who**'s own problematic history and make the audience uncomfortable by highlighting some of the Doctor's most profound flaws.

My hope is that you will read this and not see it as a definitive statement on *Hell Bent*'s feminist values, but rather as an exploration of how it explores themes of power, privilege,

---

[4] Moffat, Steven, '**Doctor Who** Series 9 Episode 12 *Hell Bent*: Green Amendments', p44.

patriarchy, and autonomy. It's the beginning of the conversation, not the end.

CHAPTER 1: A DUTY OF CARE

The Doctor's Patriarchal Flaws

> 'I had a duty of care.'
>
> [The Doctor][5]

The Doctor is our hero. He fights villains and monsters, he stops invasions and saves planets, he speaks truth to power and stands against injustice. But the Doctor is not without flaws. His acts of heroism have often required enormous acts of violence. He doesn't always live up to his promise to be 'never cruel or cowardly'[6]. And he acts in what he believes to be others' best interests, often ignoring their own wishes. In series 8, the Doctor asked himself if he was a good man[7]. Peter Capaldi described *Hell Bent* as a response to that question: 'You know the Doctor who was in last year's series? He was right. He was right to question his morality.'[8]

The Doctor of *Hell Bent* is 'an angry, off-the-rails Doctor' who has 'lost his moral compass' and is 'being selfish'[9]. And he's on a campaign to right the wrongs that were done to him in the previous two episodes. He takes down the Time Lords who trapped and tortured him in his own confession dial. And he makes the Time Lords return Clara Oswald to him by using Gallifreyan technology to extract her from her own timeline moments before her death. But

---

[5] All quotes are taken from *Hell Bent* unless otherwise stated.

[6] *The Day of the Doctor* (2013).

[7] *Into the Dalek* (2014).

[8] Cook, Benjamin, 'The Doctor and Me'. *Doctor Who Magazine* (DWM) #494.

[9] Cook, Benjamin, '*Heaven Sent* and *Hell Bent*'. DWM #493.

even as it become increasingly clear that Clara's death can't be avoided – and that by keeping her alive the Doctor could completely unravel time itself – the Doctor refuses to back down. He becomes increasingly driven to save Clara's life at any cost, even if that means ignoring her own wishes and violating her autonomy.

We've seen similar behaviours examined and challenged in previous **Doctor Who** stories, most notably around the erasure of Donna Noble's memories and the rise of the Time Lord Victorious[10]. What makes *Hell Bent* particularly interesting and unique is how it exposes and explicitly challenges the Doctor's most overbearing, patronising, and patriarchal behaviours. Even more extraordinarily, as the Doctor is made to recognise his behaviour, Clara's autonomy is respected and maintained.

Showrunner and episode writer Steven Moffat was very intentionally exploring the Doctor's flaws in *Hell Bent*. In an interview with *Doctor Who Magazine*, he stated the Doctor is 'not supposed to be a perfect cultural exemplar' because 'he's a character: he has foibles and failings that are essential to him, that drive both the drama and the comedy.' What makes him compelling as a hero is that 'he tries to be good, not [that] he already is.'

Moffat approaches the Doctor's failings primarily from a class perspective, arguing that he carries the presumptive authority and perspective of someone born to privilege and power:

> 'Every character failing he has is based on his assumption that he is cleverer, and more important, and more entitled than everyone else in the room. He's Robin Hood – he's a

---

[10] *Journey's End* (2008) and *The Waters of Mars* (2009).

slumming-it toff. He believes he's a man of the people, but he still expects the people to fetch him cups of tea. Even Christopher Eccleston's Doctor... he tries to sound like a northern bloke, but you can tell that he's basically a prince. He just has the effortless presumption of one, and the occasional blindness. His heroism is that he rises above the limitations of the worldview into which he was born, to fight for a better universe for everyone.'

There was a moment cut from *Hell Bent* that was meant to more explicitly highlight the Doctor's aristocratic presumptions, which Moffat later revealed that he deeply regretted cutting from the final episode:

'The Doctor reveals that he's reassigned the High Council to the sewers, and Ohila remarks that only an aristocrat regards honest work as punishment. That's the Doctor all over: he knows that the aristocracy must be deposed, but even in bringing it about, he reveals that he will always be one of them.'

Although Moffat's discussion of the Doctor's flaws focused on the Doctor primarily from a class perspective, he was also very aware of the impact that the gender and race of the actor portraying the Doctor could have on readings of the Doctor's behaviour in *Hell Bent*, saying, 'You certainly don't have to be a white male to play all that – though you can see why it's a decent fit.'[11] In other words, the critique Moffat is making in *Hell Bent* would be more effective precisely because it also exposes the 'effortless presumption' that the Doctor has as a result of being white and male, and examines

---

[11] Cook, Benjamin, 'The DWM Interview'. DWM #500.

how a white man uses (and potentially abuses) his power and authority.

The Doctor's patriarchal behaviour has been a longstanding and arguably essential part of the Doctor's character. In his analysis of gender representation in **Doctor Who**, Piers Britton writes that this can particularly be seen in the way the Doctor exhibits a patriarchal authority over his companions. This type of behaviour is seen throughout the series and is not confined to any particular era or regeneration. It is, rather, baked into the very foundations of the show, particularly into the way that power is distributed between the Doctor and his companions.

The very premise of the show gives 'authority to the Doctor as patriarch, and denies it to most of his companions.'[12] He controls the TARDIS (or, at the very least, he is often the only one with the knowledge and experience to attempt to fly it). Companions are often dependent on him to take them off to their adventures – or to return them home. And the Doctor controls access to the privilege of joining him in the TARDIS, and he can and has abruptly taken that privilege away. The Doctor proved to Clara how that power can be abused and manipulated in *Kill the Moon* (2014), when he abruptly abandoned her and her young student Courtney in a deadly situation when he did not approve of a proposal to destroy the Moon to save the Earth.

Britton also notes that this type of patriarchal authority extends to the way the Doctor's relationships with his companions are set up. The Doctor is generally more knowledgeable than his companions,

---

[12] Britton, Piers D, *TARDISbound: Navigating the Universes of Doctor Who*, p114.

and even companions who equal him are often placed in a position where the Doctor must temper their abilities. Companions are also often placed in a role where they must act as the Doctor's carer. The Doctor quite literally calls Clara his carer in *Into the Dalek* (2014) in a way that suggests that she must look after him **and** must manage his interactions with everybody else.

In series 9, the Doctor's claim of patriarchal authority over Clara is made much more explicit. The Doctor makes his sense of obligation for Clara's safety and wellbeing clear, repeatedly saying that he has a 'duty of care' for her.

It's an unusual phrase to use. The Collins English Dictionary defines a 'duty of care' to mean a 'legal obligation to safeguard others from harm while they are in your care'[13]. The first time the concept of a duty of care is discussed by the Doctor and Clara is in *Kill the Moon*. The Doctor takes Clara and one her students to the moon, but when the situation becomes dangerous, Clara tells the Doctor, 'Look, I have a duty of care, okay?'[14] In this situation she is clearly speaking of a professional and legal obligation to protect the life and wellbeing of a minor student in her care.

But the next two times a duty of care is discussed by the Doctor and Clara, the Doctor mentions it to suggest that he has responsibility for Clara. In *Under the Lake* (2015), the Doctor tries to encourage Clara to stay behind in the TARDIS instead of re-entering the dangerous situation outside. When she rebuffs him, he says that he felt he had to speak up because he's 'got a duty of care.'[15] She responds with

---

[13] 'Definition of "Duty of Care"'.
[14] *Kill the Moon*.
[15] *Under the Lake*.

mild exasperation, acknowledging that he feels that way without indicating whether or not she approves. But Clara shortly makes her disapproval very clear to him. In *The Girl Who Died* (2015), the Doctor again tries to convince Clara to leave a dangerous situation for her own safety, saying once again that he has a duty of care for her. Clara rebuffs him, responding: 'No you don't, because I never asked for that.'[16]

Under the Lake suggests that the Doctor has been telling Clara he has a duty of care for her for some time, but the audience does not know when this first started or what justification was given. Still, the Doctor doesn't have any clear legal or professional obligation to protect Clara. She is his friend, travelling occasionally and voluntarily with him for her own enjoyment. To assume responsibility for her is to assume a type of obligation that he plainly does not have.

The only other authority that the Doctor does have over her is the one Britton describes: a patriarchal authority to determine whether or not she can continue to travel with him and share in his dangerous adventures. Insisting that he has a duty of care absent any legal or professional obligation positions her as a dependent charge of his, in which case he has an obligation for her safety and the authority to act in what he believes to be her best interests, regardless of her wishes.

In *Under the Lake* and *The Girl Who Died*, the Doctor limits himself to requesting that Clara leave for her own safety. But in *Hell Bent*, he makes plans without her knowledge or consent that would force her to leave their adventures in the TARDIS. And it wouldn't be the first

---

[16] *The Girl Who Died.*

time the Doctor has done that to a companion.

Britton notes that one of the most unnerving ways the Doctor's patriarchal authority is presented in the show is in the 'largely unreflective celebration of his acts of intervention, and of the virtuosity with which he accomplishes them'[17]. One of the most disturbing examples of his intervention is what he does to Donna Noble in *Journey's End* (2008). After a freak accident gives her the Doctor's knowledge and intelligence, she is able to save the Doctor's life and defeat the Daleks. But all of that extra information quickly overwhelms her brain. To save her life, the Doctor telepathically erases all of the knowledge she acquired, as well as all her memories of him and their adventures together.

However, the act of erasing her memories is clearly not consensual. Throughout the scene, Donna repeatedly tells the Doctor that she does not want him to erase her memories. Even as he is erasing her memories, she is repeatedly shouting 'No!'[18] The Doctor's act is tacitly justified as being necessary to save Donna's life, and the loss of her memories is acknowledged by the Doctor and her family as being a tragedy. However, at no point is there 'the slightest acknowledgement that Donna should be able to control her own fate and her own body'[19]. The Doctor simply presumes to have the authority to override Donna's express wishes and make a decision on her behalf regarding her life and well-being.

But not all the Doctor's acts of intervention are celebrated. *The Waters of Mars* (2009) is remarkably critical of the Doctor's high-

---

[17] Britton, *TARDISbound*, p85.
[18] *Journey's End*.
[19] Britton, *TARDISbound*, p132-33.

handedness. The Doctor arrives at a human base on Mars on the eve of a major, history-altering catastrophe that kills the entire crew. It's also a fixed point in time, which places the Doctor in the unusual and difficult position of being completely unable to save them. For most of the episode, the Doctor is reluctantly resigned to leaving them to their fate.

But in a sudden change of heart, the Doctor decides to intervene and save the crew members. He acknowledges that the laws of time would normally prevent him from altering fixed points in time, but since the individuals who were in charge of those laws died (presumably the Time Lords), the Doctor claims ownership over them. And now that he has put himself in a position of authority over the laws of time, he demands that they bend to his will, shouting 'The laws of time are mine, and they will obey me!' In the nick of time, he manages to rescue the three remaining crew members.

Adelaide Brooke, the captain of the Mars mission, attempts to oppose and undermine the Doctor's actions to the best of her abilities. When the Doctor does save their lives, it is Adelaide who questions his judgement and his careless assumption that his actions will have no impact on the future. She also challenges the power he has assumed over the laws of time, telling him that no one should have the type of power the Doctor is claiming. When the Doctor tries to reassure her that he's done similar things before with 'little people' less important than Adelaide, she is furious at how he imperiously decides who is and is not important.

The Doctor, unmoved by Adelaide's criticism, declares himself 'the Time Lord Victorious'. To ensure the future occurs as it was intended to and to stop the Time Lord Victorious, Adelaide commits suicide.

Her action forces the Doctor to recognise that the Time Lord Victorious is wrong. He regret his actions, saying 'I've gone too far.'[20] Still, it is Adelaide Brooke who pays the price for the Doctor's high-handed intervention.

Hell Bent deliberately draws parallels to both the erasure of Donna's memories and the Time Lord Victorious. And both of these parallels centre around a prominent recurring character introduced earlier in series 9: Ashildr, later known simply as Me.

Ashildr was introduced in *The Girl Who Died* as a young Viking woman who provokes a war with a fierce warrior race known as the Mire. With the help of the Doctor and Clara, the Vikings force the Mire to retreat, but Ashildr is killed in the battle.

This is where the first reference to Donna is made. While the Doctor despairs over losing Ashildr in the battle, he rages against the rules that would prevent him from saving Ashildr's life. And then he remembers another time when another companion convinced him to go against the rules to save someone's life. He has a flashback to a scene from *The Fires of Pompeii* (2008) when Donna begs the 10th Doctor to save a family from the eruption of Vesuvius. Among that family was a man named Caecilius, who was portrayed by Peter Capaldi long before he was cast as the 12th Doctor. A deliberate connection is drawn between both of Capaldi's roles, with the Doctor concluding that he looks just like Caecilius 'to remind me, to hold me to the mark'[21] of Donna's demand that he save people.

The Doctor saves Ashildr's life, and in doing so makes her immortal.

---

[20] *The Waters of Mars.*
[21] *The Girl Who Died.*

But he almost immediately begins to question if he went too far. When he encounters Ashildr (who is now calling herself Me) in the next episode, *The Woman Who Lived* (2015), he finds that Me is bitter as a result of her life and angry with the Doctor for making her immortal. Me tells the Doctor: 'I live in the world you leave behind, because you abandoned me to it [...] You didn't save my life, Doctor. You trapped me inside it.'

Even when the Doctor and Me reconcile, Me makes it very clear that she distrusts the Doctor and does not approve of the way he intervenes in other's lives. She vows to be 'the patron saint of the Doctor's leftovers. While you're busy protecting this world, I'll get busy protecting it from you.'[22] So it's fitting that she's there to hold the Doctor accountable during his misguided attempt to save Clara's life.

The Doctor's plan to save Clara is the most obvious parallel to Donna's story. Although Clara has been pulled out her timeline by the Time Lords moments before her death, she isn't truly alive. She is effectively in stasis, conscious and able to interact with others but with her physical processes frozen permanently between one heartbeat and her last. But her condition is only supposed to be temporary. Her death is a fixed historical event, and if she doesn't return to the moment before her death, time could unravel.

The Doctor travels with Clara to the end of the universe, which he believes would force time to heal after having a fixed moment in time – Clara's death – altered. This should also force Clara's personal timeline to restart so she is no longer in a physical stasis. But the Doctor also believes that the Time Lords would attempt to track her

---

[22] *The Woman Who Lived.*

down and forcibly return her to the moment of her death. Because the Time Lords could track Clara by the image of the Doctor in her memories, the Doctor believes that the only way to protect her is by erasing all of her memories of him and their adventures together, exactly as he once did to Donna. The Doctor even acknowledges the parallels to what he did to Donna, saying: 'I've done it before. Usually, I do it telepathically, but this time, I've got something better.'

The tension of *Hell Bent* is ramped up by its parallel narratives. In one narrative, the audience is shown the linear events of what happens after the Doctor arrives on Gallifrey. The other narrative, which is interspersed throughout the first, shows the Doctor and Clara together in a diner in Nevada. The Doctor is telling the story of the other narrative to Clara, who apparently does not know the Doctor or remember that she was present for any of the events he is describing. This narrative style, coupled with the multiple references to Donna's fate, creates the impression that the Doctor has already gone through with his plan to erase Clara memories and that the viewer is witnessing the aftermath.

But the Doctor's attempt to save Clara doesn't go as planned. The Doctor travels as far into the future as he can, but Clara's heartbeat doesn't return. She is still frozen in the last moment of her life, and time doesn't heal. The Doctor becomes increasingly furious as it becomes clearer that his plan isn't working. When Clara asks if the Doctor might be wrong and that the universe needs her to die, he yells, 'We're standing on the last ember, the last fragment of everything that ever was. As of this moment, I'm answerable to no-one!'

That claim of power and authority is remarkably similar to the Doctor's claim over the laws of time in *The Waters of Mars*. And it's at that moment that Ashildr makes her reappearance, summoning him out of the TARDIS with an old **Doctor Who** motif – four knocks. In the 10th Doctor's final stories, the Doctor was told a prophecy in which he would hear four knocks before his death. In *The Waters of Mars*, as the Doctor is about to become the Time Lord Victorious, he asserts that this can't possibly be the moment that he dies because he doesn't hear anybody knocking. At that moment one of the infected crew members bangs three times on the door, but the Doctor stops him before he can knock a fourth time. But after Adelaide kills herself and the Doctor realises he has gone too far, he asks 'Is this it? My death? Is it time?'[23]

The fated four knocks eventually come from Donna's grandfather Wilf, who is trapped and about to be killed by radiation. When the Doctor does finally hear the four knocks that indicate his death has come, his first selfish impulse is not to save Wilf because he believes Wilf's life isn't as important as his. It's a brief moment, and the Doctor is quickly ashamed of it, saying 'I've lived too long.'[24] He accepts his fate and saves Wilf's life at the cost of his own.

Four knocks symbolise moments in the Doctor's life when his hubris, selfishness, and high-handedness have cost him and those around him dearly. So when Ashildr knocks four times at the door, the Doctor immediately recognises and acknowledges the motif, saying 'Four knocks. It's always four knocks.' It serves as a warning that he is about to go too far, and could face a horrible price if he persists.

---

[23] *The Waters of Mars.*
[24] *The End of Time* (2010).

Despite the Doctor's claim that he is answerable to no-one, there are a number of people who try to hold him accountable and attempt to intervene to protect Clara. It's a striking difference from Donna's fate in *Journey's End*. Before the Doctor erases Donna's memories against her will, he isolates her from the group by sending the rest of their friends back to their homes. No one is able to speak in her defence or intervene to stop the Doctor. Notably, all of those who speak up on Clara's behalf are — or have been in previous and future regenerations — women.

Clara's first advocate is the General. When the Doctor uses the extraction chamber to pull Clara out of her timeline, he's reluctant to explain what he's done to her. The General repeatedly insists that Clara has a right to know what has happened to her, and when the Doctor fails to fully explain, the General steps in to provide the necessary explanations himself.

Ohila is Clara's next advocate. She had been critical of the Doctor's actions from the very beginning, particularly of his decision to banish Rassilon and the High Council from Gallifrey. But when the Doctor is about to take Clara off of Gallifrey, she gives her most pointed denunciation of him yet. When the Doctor claims that the universe owes him Clara's survival, Ohila shoots back that the universe doesn't owe him anything, and that his selfish actions will only hurt Clara.

And then, of course, there is Ashildr. When she confronts the Doctor at the end of the universe, she chastises him for refusing to accept Clara's death – and for how he plans to alter her to keep her alive. Ashildr advocates repeatedly for Clara's autonomy and bodily integrity, telling the Doctor that 'We have no right to change who

25

[Clara] was.' When the Doctor tells Ashildr that he is going to erase Clara's memories and leave her on Earth, Ashildr points out that Clara may not want him to do that. She also asks him if he plans on telling Clara that he is going to erase her memories before he does it, and she follows him into the TARDIS to see that he does.

Clara's final and best advocate, however, is herself. And when the Doctor finally, reluctantly tells Clara what he plans to do, she forcefully defends her autonomy and challenges the Doctor's presumption to make decisions on her behalf.

The Doctor starts the conversation with the clear presumption that his plan to erase Clara's memories and leave her on Earth is best for her. He avoids telling her the complete truth about what he intends to do to her for as long as possible, refusing to say outright what the consequences will be for her. As Clara presses him to reveal that he wants to erase her memories, he replies 'Clara, just listen to me.' He regards her objections as an obstacle to be overcome instead of a clear sign that he shouldn't proceed.

Earlier in *Hell Bent* the Doctor said again that he has a 'duty of care' for Clara. Now, as he tries to justify his actions, he again says that he has only been trying to keep Clara safe. And in his mind, it is the logical extension of his duty of care towards her. He has presumed the obligation to keep her safe, and because she has died under his watch, he now has the obligation to save her life by any means necessary.

Both the Doctor's impulse and his execution are paternalistic. Clara made it clear in earlier episodes that she did not ask for the Doctor to assume a duty of care for her and repeats herself again in *Hell Bent*, saying 'I've never asked you for that, ever.' By continuing to insist he does have that type of obligation, he indicates that he doesn't trust her to make her own decisions regarding her safety and repeatedly disregards her own explicit wishes. And in *Hell Bent*, he assumes the authority to make decisions on her behalf, never once considering what Clara wants or asking for her input on his plan.

But when the moment comes for the Doctor to erase Clara's memories, Clara has the opportunity to do what Donna never could – forcefully and vocally advocate for the right to her own autonomy. In one of the most powerful moments of the story, Clara tells the Doctor:

> 'These have been the best years of my life, and they are mine. Tomorrow is promised to no one, Doctor, but I insist upon my past. I am entitled to that. It's mine.'

That statement is not a request – it's a demand. Clara demands that the Doctor respect her right to make her own decision about her life and her death. Her memories and her life are hers alone, and so the decision about what could or should be done to save her life must also be hers. She demands for her autonomy and mental integrity to be respected. Unlike Donna, there will be no erasing of her memories without her explicit permission.

Although there is nothing indicating that this was intentional on Moffat's part, it's hard not to read this story as anything other than a critique on the erasure of Donna's memories. *Hell Bent* is not the 'largely unreflective celebration' of the Doctor's intervention that Britton critiqued. It is, rather, a deeply reflective critique of the Doctor's paternalism and the sense of patriarchal authority that enables him to intervene in his companions' lives.

Britton noted that there was no acknowledgment that Donna should be able to control her own mind and fate. That is partly what makes Clara's statement so powerful – it feels like everything Donna should have been able to say, but couldn't. Donna's fear and desperation are so clear when she begs the Doctor not to erase her memories, and the tragedy of her loss is acknowledged. But it is never made clear how wrong the Doctor's actions are, and just how much of a violation it was to erase Donna's memories without her consent.

Not only is there an acknowledgement that Clara should be able to control her mind and her fate, her declaration that she should is the moment on which the whole episode turns. It's only after Clara's demand that the Doctor finally realises just how wrong his actions have been. He has become something far more terrifying than the Time Lord Victorious – he has become the Hybrid.

Just like in *The Waters of Mars* and *The End of Time* (2010), the Doctor spends series 9 running away from a prophecy. This prophecy concerns the coming of a creature known as the Hybrid, which is thought to be crossbred between two warrior races and will one day 'stand in the ruins of Gallifrey, unravel the web of time and destroy a billion billion hearts to heal its own.' It is the Time Lords' fear of the Hybrid which drives them to trap the Doctor on Earth – a plot which accidentally results in Clara's death – and torture him in his own confession dial to force him to reveal what he knows.

But instead of preventing the Hybrid's coming, their actions precipitate it. Ashildr proposes that the Hybrid is the Doctor and Clara. Instead of a crossbreed between two warrior races, the Hybrid is instead the result of the relationship between 'a passionate and powerful Time Lord and a young woman so very similar to him.' In *Doctor Who Magazine* Moffat confirmed that she was correct, saying that 'Clara was the precise motivator that would drive the Doctor to an extreme that was dangerous for all time and space [...]the coming of the Hybrid would be the result of their association.'[25] But while the Hybrid is the result of their relationship, it is the Doctor who takes sole responsibility. He confesses to Clara: 'I went too far. I broke all my own rules. I became the Hybrid.'

While Clara is a part of the creation of the Hybrid, it is the Doctor's actions which bring on the Hybrid. He destroys billions of his own hearts in the confession dial to get to Gallifrey and force the Time Lords to bring Clara back. Once he has her, he is the one that takes her to the ruins of Gallifrey. And he is the one who is determined to save her life at any cost, over her repeated objections, even when he knows that the result of saving her life could unravel time.

Clara is the object of the Doctor's fixation, but she is not the one who crosses boundaries. The Hybrid is the result of their association, but Clara and the Doctor do not share equal responsibility for its creation. It is primarily a reflection of the Doctor's flaws. The Hybrid is his own presumption of patriarchal authority and paternalism.

What happens next subverts every expectation the narrative has been building. To stop the Hybrid and prevent the situation from escalating further, the Doctor and Clara both use the neural block together. Random chance will determine who will have their memories erased. In a shocking turnabout, it is the Doctor who loses his memories of Clara. During the entire scene in the diner, it was the Doctor who couldn't recognise Clara.

It's a fitting consequences for his actions as the Hybrid. For breaking

---

[25] Moffat, Steven, 'Ask Steven Moffat'. DWM #504.

his own rules, he endures the same fate he wanted for Clara – deprived of his memories and left back on Earth without his TARDIS. But while the Doctor is fallen, he is not irredeemable. The Hybrid was a reflection and amplification of the worst of the Doctor's flaws, ones which he recognised and faced the consequences for. After the Doctor talks with Clara in the diner, she returns his TARDIS to him and leaves him with a final reminder: 'Run you clever boy and be a Doctor.'

And Clara, still stuck in a physical stasis but with her mind and memories intact, gets to determine what she does next. Her autonomy is respected and maintained. She's free to decide how she will spend the rest of her life and when and how she will return to the moment of her death. With a stolen TARDIS and Ashildr as her companion, she decides she will eventually return to Gallifrey so that the Time Lords can put return her to the moment of her death. But before she does, she'll take advantage of her functional immortality first, and have a few more adventures along the way.

CHAPTER 2: THE GUNFIGHTER

The Western Genre in Doctor Who

> 'Defocussed, a figure approaching, like a gunfighter coming in from the desert.'
>
> [*Hell Bent* script][26]

Doctor Who loves a good Stetson. From the very beginning, **Doctor Who** writers have been adapting and drawing upon the western genre for their stories. Sometimes, it's for the pure joy of putting the Doctor in a historical setting and a big hat. But even when there's not a single Stetson to be found, multiple **Doctor Who** episodes draw on the genre's deeper thematic elements, including culture clashes, struggles over resources, and vigilante violence. *Hell Bent* is directly influenced by western films, but unlike previous forays into the genre, it takes a markedly different approach to the Doctor's willingness to engage in gun violence.

The two most prominent examples of **Doctor Who**'s western stories are *The Gunfighters* (1966) and *A Town Called Mercy* (2012). Both of these stories are direct adaptations of the genre, set in the western American frontier in the 19th century. As actual adaptation, their approaches vastly differ. In his study of **Doctor Who**'s adaption of the western genre, Marcus Harmes remarked that *Gunfighters* is an 'overt parody of western conventions'[27], while *Mercy* takes the conventions more seriously, even as those conventions are undercut

---

[26] Moffat, '*Hell Bent*: Green Amendments', p3.
[27] Harmes, Marcus K, *Doctor Who and the Art of Adaptation: 50 Years of Storytelling*, p127.

or blended with classic science-fiction conventions.

Central to both of these stories is the role of gunfighters and gunslingers. Although they are a prominent feature of the genre, the definition of a 'gunfighter' can be broad and nebulous. *The BFI Companion to the Western* less than helpfully states that 'every western hero is in a sense a gunfighter; a conflict with firearms is the almost invariable conclusion to a western film.'[28] The western film's gunfighter can be a heroic figure fighting for justice, a 'two-gun Galahad whose pistols are always at the service of those in trouble.'[29] But a gunfighter can also be an outlaw 'who lives by the gun'[30], or a hired gun whose services are available to the highest bidder. Their role in westerns is flexible, as is their relative morality.

The Gunfighters directly inserts the Doctor, Dodo, and Steven into one of the most notorious gunfighter stories of the genre: the shootout between the Clantons and the Earps at the OK Corral. However, the Doctor and his companions don't make very impressive gunfighters, and their interactions with guns are mostly played for comedic affect. When they arrive in Tombstone, Arizona, Steven plays at being a gunfighter and almost immediately fumbles his gun[31]. When the Doctor is locked up in jail after being mistaken for the notorious gunfighter Doc Holliday, Steven smuggles him a gun so he can break out. But the Doctor, rather horrified by the whole idea, immediately hands the gun over to Sheriff Wyatt Earp,

---

[28] Buscombe, Edward, ed, *The BFI Companion to the Western*, p132.
[29] Rosa, Joseph G, *The Gunfighter: Man or Myth?*, p4.
[30] Buscombe, *BFI Companion to the Western*, p132.
[31] 'A Holiday for the Doctor' (*The Gunfighters* episode 1, 1966).

saying: 'I wonder, would you mind looking after it for me?'[32]

A Town Called Mercy is a much darker story that grapples with the complicated role that gunfighters play in westerns. The Doctor travels with Amy and Rory to a town in the American west under siege by a cyborg the locals call 'the Gunslinger.' They later discover that the Gunslinger is seeking justice for the crimes committed against him by an alien named Kahler Jex, who is being harboured by the town. The Gunslinger is alternately seen as a villain, victim, and vigilante.

As Harmes notes, the Doctor's role in *Mercy* is morally ambiguous. At first, the Doctor is willing to hand over Kahler Jex to the Gunslinger to be killed. Almost like a vigilante gunfighter himself, the Doctor marches Kahler Jex out of town at gunpoint. Amy convinces him that his actions are morally repugnant, but before they can all return to safety, the Gunslinger arrives and accidentally shoots the town's Sheriff.

At this point the Doctor's role in the story shifts. He takes over the duties of the Sheriff and works to preserve order in the town. And while he occasionally carries a gun, he never uses it. When the town forms a mob to hand over Kahler Jex to the Gunslinger, the Doctor displays a gun but doesn't draw it. The Doctor even admits to the leader of the mob that he would certainly lose in a quick draw – a distinctive talent of nearly every gunfighter – and instead convinces the mob that gun violence is not the way to resolve the situation. The climax of the story invokes another western trope as the Doctor and the Gunslinger face off for a gun battle at high noon. But instead of drawing a gun, the Doctor draws his sonic screwdriver, setting off

---

[32] 'Don't Shoot the Pianist' (*The Gunfighters* episode 2, 1966).

a clever plan intended to avoid gun violence.

Though the Doctor borrows the gunfighter's style and swagger, in *Gunfighters* and *Mercy* he eschews their most defining tool: guns. The Doctor has always had a complicated relationship with firearms. He has occasionally used guns against monsters, villains, and overly complicated bits of machinery. But he has also repeatedly opposed the use of guns, often framing them as something antithetical to the way he operates.

In *Gunfighters* the first Doctor tells Wyatt Earp: 'People keep giving me guns and do I wish they wouldn't.'[33] In *The Robots of Death* (1977), the fourth Doctor tells Leela she won't need to carry a gun by saying: 'I never carry weapons. If people see you mean them no harm, they never hurt you.' In *Doctor Who* (1996), he is happy to use a gun to threaten his own safety, but not that of others. In *The Doctor's Daughter* (2008), the 10th Doctor holds a gun to the head of a murderer as if he intended to kill him for his crime, before suddenly dropping the gun and saying 'I never would. Have you got that? I. Never. Would.' And when the 11th Doctor drives Kahler Jex out of town at gunpoint in *Mercy*, Amy forces him to reconsider his behaviour by reminding him that 'this is not how we roll, and you know it.'[34]

And although the Doctor has occasionally picked up a gun, guns aren't a regular part of his outfit or equipment. Showrunner Steven Moffat argued that the Doctor's lack of a gun makes him particularly unique and important as a hero, saying: 'When they made this

---

[33] 'Don't Shoot the Pianist'.
[34] *A Town Called Mercy*.

particular hero, they didn't give him a gun. They gave him a screwdriver to fix things.'[35] The Doctor's use of his sonic screwdriver in place of a gun – such as was seen in the climatic scene in *Mercy* – is an essential and defining part of his character.

All of which makes the framing of the Doctor as a gunfighter and his use of a gun to intentionally kill a fellow Time Lord in *Hell Bent* particularly interesting. Instead of eschewing gun violence to achieve his goals, he embraces it.

Unlike *Gunfighters* or *Mercy*, *Hell Bent* is not a direct adaptation of an American western, but it draws upon the same visual and thematic elements. Most of the story takes place in locations that are evocative of the western American frontier. The diner where the Doctor meets Clara sits in an empty desert in contemporary Nevada. The action on Gallifrey begins out in the Drylands, where we see broad desert vistas, wooden barns, and residents who wear simple farmland garb instead of the robes and headdresses of the Gallifreyan elite.

Director Rachel Talalay told *Doctor Who Magazine* that because Steven Moffat had written the first act as a western, she turned to iconic western director Sergio Leone's work for inspiration for *Hell Bent*'s western visuals[36]. Her collection of visual references for the episode includes frames from several of Leone's films, including *A Fistful of Dollars* (1964), *The Good, the Bad, and the Ugly* (1966) and

---

[35] 'The Doctor the Ultimate Hero: Steven Moffat on the *Eleventh Hour* Panel – **Doctor Who**'.

[36] Cook, Benjamin, '*Heaven Sent* and *Hell Bent*'.

Once Upon a Time in the West (1968)[37].

Leone was known for 'alternating between stunning wide-screen panoramas and extreme close-ups of his actors' faces and eyes, often within the same shot.'[38] This style can be particularly seen in the opening scene of *Once Upon a Time in the West*, where three hired guns stake out an isolated train station to ambush a mysterious harmonica-playing man. Many of Talalay's visual references come from this long, drawn-out scene. Her screenshots include extreme close-ups of the hired guns' faces, and wide shots with the four figures facing off across the barren landscape.

You can see these visuals reflected in the visuals of *Hell Bent*'s first act. Talalay would have liked to shoot *Hell Bent* in cinematic widescreen, but found other ways within the production limitations to pay homage to Leone's iconic format[39]. We frequently see the Doctor's figure isolated against panoramic shots of the Nevadan and Gallifreyan landscapes, mimicking the feel (if not the exact aspect ratio) of a widescreen shot. As the Doctor walks across the Gallifreyan desert, these wide shots are interspersed with sudden, extreme close-ups on the Doctor's face as he surveys the landscape and his opponents.

There are other cues thematically positioning the Doctor as the gunfighter of this tale. Immediately following the title credits, we see

---

[37] Talalay, Rachel, email interview with the author, 10 February 2018.
[38] Edwards, Dan, 'Sergio Leone'.
[39] Leone's westerns conform to the standard aspect ratio of 2.35:1 for cinema films, significantly wider than the modern TV standard of 16:9.

the Doctor's lone figure trudging across a desert, our vision of him blurred by a shimmering heat wave. The script describes the Doctor's approach as being similar to 'a gunfighter coming in from the desert.'[40] Later, as the Doctor discards his red velvet coat for a simple black jacket, the script describes the scene this way: 'The Doctor is checking himself out in the mirror. He's changed – now wearing the same farmhand garb as everyone else (**as close to Shane as we dare.**)' [emphasis added][41].

Shane (1953) is one of the most highly regarded films of the western genre, ranking third on the American Film Institute's list of top 10 western films[42]. It is also regarded as one of the most quintessential gunfighter stories of the genre, with *The BFI Companion to the Western* highlighting it as one of the movies that best explored the incompatibility of a gunfighters' trade with the values of civilised society[43]. The movie opens as Shane, the eponymous gunfighter, rides into a isolated Wyoming settlement, where he attempts to leave behind his violent past to become a farmhand. But when a cattle rancher steps up a campaign of intimidation to force homesteaders off their land, Shane feels compelled to use his unique and deadly skill set to defend the family that took him in.

Clothing transitions mark important character developments in *Shane* just as they do in *Hell Bent*, although their use is inverted in *Hell Bent*. Shane arrives at the farmstead wearing a buckskin fringe jacket with a six-gun revolver strapped to a silver-plated belt, looking every bit the part of a deadly gunfighter. When he decides to stay on

---

[40] Moffat, '*Hell Bent*: Green Amendments', p3.
[41] Moffat, '*Hell Bent*: Green Amendments', p10.
[42] 'AFI's 10 Top 10: Top 10 Western'.
[43] Buscombe, *BFI Companion to the Western*, p297.

the homestead, he goes into town and buys a new shirt and slacks – farmhand garb. And when Shane decides to face the cattle rancher and his crew, he discards his farmhand clothes and dons the buckskin jacket, belt, and revolver, marking himself as a gunfighter again before the shooting begins.

In *Hell Bent*, the Doctor arrives on the farmstead carrying his red velvet coat, a classic **Doctor Who** costume that is reminiscent of coats worn by both the third and fourth Doctors and which Clara describes later in the episode as being 'very Doctory.' The Doctor discards this coat and dons the simple black jacket before beginning his campaign against the Time Lords, which begins with him driving Rassilon and the High Council off of Gallifrey and culminates in the Doctor shooting a fellow Time Lord. Like Shane's act of donning the buckskin fringe jacket, the Doctor's act of discarding his red velvet coat and donning the simple black jacket serves as a visual marker that he has given up any attempt to resolve the situation without violence.

In *Shane*, the conflict ends after Shane shoots and kills the cattle rancher, but Shane finds no redemption after the violence. He remarks that 'there's no living with [...] a killing. There's no going back from it.'[44] He then rides off towards the horizon, still wearing his gunfighter outfit, branding him as a man trapped by violence.

But the Doctor does find redemption after violence. Once the conflict has ended, the Doctor returns to his TARDIS and finds his red velvet coat alongside a handwritten message from Clara saying: 'Run you clever boy and be a Doctor.' And after he puts on the coat, the TARDIS provides him with a brand new sonic screwdriver – the very

---

[44] *Shane.*

tool that Steven Moffat remarked is the Doctor's alternative to a gun. Both items visually mark him as the man who abhors guns and violence again.

There are other narrative similarities between *Hell Bent* and *Shane*. Consider the moment that the Doctor shoots the General. It is sudden and violent – and very abnormal for the Doctor. The script describes the scene as such:

> 'And [the Doctor] turns and punches the General so hard in the face. The General spins, flailing. In the same motion – so expert – the Doctor snatches the gun from the falling General. Now levels it at him. **(This action should be swift and scarily efficient – a tiny, disconcerting glimpse of the War Doctor, and what he was once like.)**' [emphasis added][45]

There's something akin to a quick draw in the way this scene is framed. The Doctor's action as he snatches the General's gun from his holster is quick, efficient, and deadly effective. It seems incongruous coming from this Doctor, but there's a hint of his violent past, a previous regeneration that was much more effective and comfortable with weapons.

Compare this scene to a similar quick draw scene from *Shane*. For a movie about a gunfighter, *Shane* has surprisingly few scenes where Shane actually fires his gun. It's kept wrapped up and out of sight for the vast majority of the movie, and he only fires it twice – once in the final confrontation with the cattle rancher, and once where he teaches a young boy on the homestead how to quick draw. Still wearing his farmhand garb, Shane straps on his belt and holster and

---

[45] Moffat, '*Hell Bent*: Green Amendments', p27.

shows the boy the quickest, most efficient way to draw a gun. At the boy's insistence, Shane demonstrates how to quick draw by drawing his own weapon and firing. It seems almost incongruous to see a man in farmhand garb strap on a silver-plated belt and holster and fire a revolver, but there's a haunted look on Shane's face that reminds the audience that he has a unseen history of violence.

Look a bit deeper and you'll find even more similarities between the Doctor and Shane. In a story littered with characters who use their proficiency with guns to harass and intimidate those without any defence, Shane stands out for using his power sparingly, and only to defend others. But what compels him to do it? He receives no benefit, no reward. The movie ends as he rides into the night out of town in a self-imposed exile.

In his review of *Shane*, Roger Ebert wrote that there's 'a little of the samurai in him, and the medieval knight. He has a code.' But are Shane's actions a one-time act, motived only by the sheer injustice of the situation? Ebert casts doubt on that, proposing that:

> 'if we were to follow Shane from town to town, I suspect we would find ritual reenactments of the pattern he's trapped in [...] he interests himself in another man's quarrel, introduces himself as "a friend," displays his six-gun and essentially chooses to get involved in a scenario that's none of his business and will lead to an ending we suspect he's seen many times before.'[46]

Does that sound like anyone we might know? The Doctor lives by a

---

[46] Roger Ebert, 'Great Movie: *Shane*'.

code as well, a promise to be 'never cruel or cowardly' and to 'never give up, never give in.'[47] He wanders from place to place, 'just passing through, helping out.'[48] And if you'd ask him why, he'd say 'I'm the Doctor, and I save people.'[49] But there's a part of him that needs to be intervening and interfering. He's trapped in a pattern, too.

And in the end, both Shane and the Doctor choose a form of self-imposed exile as punishment for their actions. As he leaves town, Shane says that the act of killing someone is 'a brand. A brand that sticks.'[50] The Doctor has carried many similar brands when his actions have resulted in death – the Oncoming Storm[51], the Time Lord Victorious[52], the Warrior[53], and now the Hybrid. And as he is about to have his memory of Clara erased, sending him into a brief exile without a TARDIS or a companion, he says: 'It's okay. I went too far [...] This is right. I accept it.'

The 12th Doctor does eventually end his exile and triumphantly returns to his TARDIS, shedding all the markers of the gunfighter and reclaiming his role as the Doctor again. But as he rides off into space, with one more season until his eventual regeneration, it does seem as if he's only at the beginning of the pattern again.

---

[47] *The Day of the Doctor.*
[48] *Death in Heaven* (2014).
[49] *The Girl Who Died.*
[50] *Shane.*
[51] *The Parting of the Ways* (2005).
[52] *The Waters of Mars.*
[53] 'The Night of the Doctor' (2013).

CHAPTER 3: CLARA WHO?

A Different Kind of Departure

'Why can't I be like you?'

[Clara, *Face the Raven* (2015)]

Hell Bent is Clara's departure story. It is also her origin story. And both stories break the mould for modern companions. The story of how Clara Oswald leaves the Doctor breaks a trend where the Doctor's companions are returned (frequently without their consent) to the domestic lives they had been trying to escape. Clara is allowed to leave on her own terms, for the life she wants to live. But *Hell Bent* is also the story of how Clara becomes the Doctor – not just someone who is **like** the Doctor, but a character who has the same power within the narrative as he does.

Clara was always a character who was never content to play second fiddle to the Doctor. When Steven Moffat first wrote the character, he imagined her as a young, contemporary, female version of the Doctor, who would be 'terribly clever' but also have 'a wayward ego', reflecting both the Doctor's strengths and flaws. And like the Doctor, she isn't particularly suited to living an everyday, domestic life. Moffat said that Clara 'doesn't feel like she particularly fits in the world that she lives in' and that 'she's not really very good at living a normal life.'[54]

These similarities between the Doctor and Clara were repeatedly drawn out in series 8. She grows more confident, more clever, and

---

[54] Anderson, Kyle, 'Steven Moffat on Clara Becoming the Doctor in **Doctor Who** Series 8'.

more willing to take a leading role during their adventures. In *Flatline* (2014) she actually assumes the Doctor's role after he becomes trapped in the TARDIS. She introduces herself as 'the Doctor,' finds a companion to assist her, and attempts to protect a group of humans after they are attacked by a group of mysterious aliens. When the Doctor is completely cut off from Clara, she determines on her own how to free him from the TARDIS and defeat the aliens.

The most obvious parallel is drawn between the two at the beginning of *Death in Heaven* (2014). After being cornered by a Cyberman, Clara comes up with a clever way to trick it into keeping her alive – she pretends that she actually **is** the Doctor. This pronouncement leads directly into the title credits, which has been shifted to give Jenna Coleman the treatment that Peter Capaldi receives as the lead actor who portrays the Doctor. Her name is shown before Capaldi's, and her eyes replace his in the background of the time vortex.

According to Moffat, this swap was intended as a joke, but it was grounded in his Doctorish characterisation of Clara. Moffat was inspired to swap Coleman and Capaldi's names because the character of Clara 'has no idea she's number two in the credits.' Clara views herself as the protagonist of her own story, not a sidekick or an accessory to the Doctor's story. If you asked Clara to name the TV show she was a part of, she wouldn't think the show would be named **Doctor Who**, because 'she thinks the show is called "Clara".'[55]

We also see the increasing tension between her attempts to live a normal, domestic life on Earth while also travelling with the Doctor. During series 8 she begins dating a fellow teacher, Danny Pink, but

---

[55] Anderson, 'Steven Moffat on Clara'.

she finds it incredible difficult to maintain her new relationship in between her adventures with the Doctor. In *The Caretaker* (2014) there is a montage showing her increasingly desperate attempts to keep her two lives separate. When an alien threatens the school that they both teach at, Danny discovers her secret life with the Doctor. He's upset that Clara didn't tell him about the Doctor, and disapproves of both the Doctor and the dangerous adventures that they have together.

Although Danny reluctantly accepts the Doctor's role in Clara's life, the tension between Clara's domestic life with Danny and her adventures with the Doctor increases. She lies to Danny and tells him that she has stopped travelling with the Doctor in *Mummy on the Orient Express* (2014), and she lies repeatedly in *Flatline* and *In the Forest of the Night* (2014) to maintain that first lie.

Their relationship ultimately comes to an end in *Dark Water / Death in Heaven* (2014). Clara attempts to save their relationship by telling Danny the truth about her travels with the Doctor – and by telling him that she loves him. But just as she begins to have that conversation with Danny, he is killed in a car accident. Despite the Doctor and Clara's best efforts to bring him back to life, he ultimately sacrifices himself and saves another person's life in place of his own.

Clara's failed relationship with Danny is, according to Moffat, more proof of her similarities to the Doctor. Because her relationship to Danny is 'just a little bit less exciting than running off in the blue box'[56], Clara gives their relationship less attention than it needs to survive. Ultimately, she finds a domestic life on Earth, with a job and a boyfriend, less interesting and fulfilling than travelling with the

---

[56] Anderson, 'Steven Moffat on Clara'.

Doctor.

As we move into series 9, the similarities between the Doctor and Clara become even more pronounced. With Danny gone, Clara's everyday life on Earth recedes even further into the background of the show, making only brief appearances in *The Magician's Apprentice*, *The Woman Who Lived*, and *The Zygon Invasion* (all 2015).

Clara and the Doctor also become increasingly frustrated and concerned with how each of them are handling travelling together in the TARDIS. In *Under the Lake*, the Doctor becomes concerned by how eager Clara is to run out into danger and how little she has to tie her back to Earth, like another relationship. He's concerned that she's gone 'native' to life in the TARDIS, saying, 'Look, there's a whole dimension in here, but there's only room for one me.'[57] She shares too much of his own reckless eagerness for his own comfort.

Clara, meanwhile, is frustrated by how high-handed the Doctor can still be when determining when and how they travel and intervene in the events around them. At the conclusion of one adventure in *The Girl Who Died*, while the Doctor and Clara are debating whether or not they did enough to protect a threatened population, Clara says 'You're always talking about what you can and can't do but you never tell me the rules.' She also begins expressing her frustration with the Doctor's attempts to have her leave dangerous situations by saying he has a 'duty of care'[58].

The ultimate culmination of Clara's increasing similarities to the

---

[57] *Under the Lake.*
[58] *The Girl Who Died.*

Doctor is her death in *Face the Raven*. The Doctor and Clara are called to help their friend Rigsy, who has been branded with a chronolock. When the chronolock reaches zero, a creature will be released that will kill him. The Doctor and Clara's investigation of how and why Rigsy was given the chronolock leads them to an alien refugee community in the heart of London run by Ashildr, now going by the name Mayor Me. Unbeknownst to them, Ashildr has, at the direction of the Time Lords, placed the chronolock on Rigsy in order to lure the Doctor into a trap.

During their investigation, Clara learns that the chronolock can be given from one person to another, and she tells Rigsy to give it to her. Ashildr has placed Clara under her personal protection, so Clara reasons that if they aren't able to convince Ashildr to voluntarily remove the chronolock from Rigsy and spare his life, Clara can force her to remove the chronolock because Ashildr has promised that she will come to no harm. Clara characterises this plan as a strategic gambit to buy them more time, framing it explicitly as 'Doctor 101' – the basic strategy you learn while travelling with and observing the Doctor. 'Doctor 201', as she tells Rigsy, is to never reveal your plan, which is why she refuses to tell the Doctor what they are about to do.

What Clara doesn't know is that by transferring the chronolock, she's cancelled out Ashildr's ability to remove it at all, irrevocably condemning Clara to die. When Ashildr reveals this, Clara still looks for a clever way out, telling the Doctor: 'We always fix it.' The Doctor tries to find a solution, threatening to destroy Ashildr and her refugee community if she doesn't find a way to spare Clara's life. At this point Clara stops the Doctor, and accepts that there's nothing that can be done to save her life.

In the moments before her death, the Doctor laments that he let Clara get too reckless. Clara angrily retorts: 'Why shouldn't I be so reckless? You're reckless all the bloody time. Why can't I be like you?' In her mind, all she had done was behave exactly as the Doctor had, by accepting a certain amount of risk in order to implement a strategic plan that could save everyone. This was 'Doctor 101'. But instead of saving a life, she needlessly sacrificed her own. The consequences seem disproportionate to any action they've taken.

The Doctor replies: 'there's nothing special about me. I am nothing, but I'm less breakable than you.'[59] To an extent, this is true. From an intradiegetic perspective, the Doctor is an alien who is remarkably physically resilient and able to survive things that an average human would not be able to survive. And if he can't survive it, he is able to regenerate into an entirely new body.

But from an extradiegetic perspective, the Doctor is unable to die in **Doctor Who** because he is the protagonist and title character. Companions regularly come and go, and even die[60], but there is no **Doctor Who** without the Doctor. So while he might be put in mortal danger, and has regularly regenerated while near death, he will never be permanently killed because the narrative of the show will not survive without him.

When I first reviewed *Face the Raven*, before Clara returned in *Hell Bent*, I wrote that 'although [Clara] is the protagonist of her own story – the star of "Clara Who" – she isn't actually the lead character

---

[59] *Face the Raven*.
[60] Adric's death in *Earthshock* (1982) is a particularly notable example.

of this show.'[61] So while Clara might act like the star of her own show, like Moffat says, she won't be protected from the consequences of her actions by the narrative of the show in the same way the Doctor might be, because **Doctor Who**'s narrative can continue without her. The Doctor might as well have said that he's less expendable than Clara.

And yet, Clara does survive. Her return in *Hell Bent* explicitly parallels key points of the Doctor's origin story, and she increasingly begins to take on key signifiers of the Doctor's identity and personality. In a preview of *Hell Bent*, Steven Moffat said: 'Clara is no longer the apprentice; she's sort of become the Doctor – she's made her way right to the top of the hill – and this finale is the fallout from that.'[62]

The key thing that has been physically changed about Clara after the Doctor pulls her out of her timeline moments before her death is that she is practically immortal. She is physically frozen in time. She'll never age, and similarly to the Doctor, she won't die under normal circumstances. She is now, as the Doctor might say, less breakable than she was.

Once Clara has been pulled from her timeline, she and the Doctor have to evade capture by the Time Lords. And so they steal a TARDIS to escape Gallifrey. This parallels the Doctor's own origin story, in which he stole his TARDIS in order to leave Gallifrey. Clara draws that explicit parallel for the Time Lords, telling them: 'The Doctor is back on Gallifrey [...] What do you think he's going to do now? Why, he's stealing a TARDIS and running away!'

---

[61] Franke, Alyssa, 'Whovian Feminism Reviews *Face the Raven*'.
[62] Cook, Benjamin, '*Heaven Sent* and *Hell Bent*'.

Once the Doctor and Clara part, Clara takes possession of the newly stolen TARDIS. It is almost identical in internal appearance to the first Doctor's TARDIS, narratively positioning Clara at the beginning of her own journey as a quasi-Doctor figure. She also shortly discovers that the chameleon circuit may not be working properly, and that the exterior of the TARDIS may be stuck in the first disguise it took when it landed on Earth – an American diner. This is another parallel to the beginning of the Doctor's narrative. In *An Unearthly Child* (1963), the Doctor was shocked to discover that his TARDIS remained disguised as a police call box even once it had been transported away from Earth[63].

Clara's actions throughout *Hell Bent* parallel the Doctor's in other ways as well. When she realises that the Doctor intends to erase her memories, she steals his sonic sunglasses (which have been used in place of his more traditional sonic screwdriver throughout series 9) and uses them to sabotage the device he intends to use. She tells the Doctor that she 'reversed the polarity', a phrase that was first used in **Doctor Who** by the third Doctor and has been used regularly since then, most recently by the 12th Doctor in *The Girl Who Died*.

The Doctor himself also positions Clara as his successor – or even his replacement. As he is about to lose his memories of her, he passes on many of the same instructions or promises he has made to himself in the past. He tells her to never eat pears, a reference to a deleted scene from *Human Nature* (2007) where the 10th Doctor instructs Martha to never let him eat pears[64]. He tells her to run, echoing both a command that the Doctor frequently gives and his

---

[63] 'The Cave of Skulls' (*An Unearthly Child* episode 2, 1963).

[64] Britt, Ryan, 'Doctor Who Hating Pears Was a Deep-Cut Easter Egg'.

own description of the way he travels through time and space. The Doctor also tells Clara to 'Never be cruel and never be cowardly.' This phrase was first used onscreen in *The Day of the Doctor* (2013), where the Doctor tells Clara that he chose the name 'the Doctor' as a promise to never be cruel or cowardly.

This moment is made all the more powerful considering how far the Doctor has fallen over the course of this story, and indeed, the entire season as he has become the Hybrid. Over the course of this season he has gradually lost some of the most prominent visual signifiers of the Doctor. His sonic screwdriver was destroyed in *The Magician's Apprentice*, his TARDIS was taken from him in *Face the Raven*, and by the beginning of *Hell Bent* he has discarded his Doctory red velvet coat. To rescue Clara, he shoots a fellow Time Lord in cold blood with a stolen gun. And as Ohila notes, he has 'broken every code [he] ever lived by.' Even the Doctor eventually recognises how far he has fallen. And so, when he is unable to live up to his own code to be the Doctor, he positions Clara within his own narrative to be the Doctor in her own right.

Of course, the Doctor is not permanently fallen. He eventually regains his velvet coat and his TARDIS, and the TARDIS even gives him a brand new sonic screwdriver. But Clara is not made to give up what she has acquired once the Doctor is redeemed again. She leaves with a TARDIS and companion of her own, with a nearly eternal lifespan ahead of her. She accepts that she'll have to return to Gallifrey eventually to be returned to the moment of her death, but she decides to have a few more adventures along the way. Clara tells Ashildr that they are going to 'Gallifrey [...] The long way round,' echoing the Doctor's own statement in *The Day of the Doctor* that he has always been heading back towards his home, 'the long way round.'[65]

The final shot of the episode shows Clara's TARDIS and the Doctor's TARDIS spinning off into space, heading in separate directions. The narrative of **Doctor Who** continues to follow the Doctor in his police box, because he is the protagonist of this show. But there is the sense that if the camera panned to follow the American diner, we might see a television show called "Clara Who" instead.

Clara's narrative, in addition to deliberately reflecting the Doctor's, carries that same powerful sense that there might also be an infinite number of stories within it. After *Hell Bent* aired there was even conversation about how well-suited Clara and Ashildr's future adventures in the TARDIS would be for a spin-off series[66]. It has yet to happen, but the potential still remains for those stories to be explored in novels, comic books, or Big Finish audios.

While we could interpret *Hell Bent* as Clara's origin story, it was, in the most technical sense, her departure story from **Doctor Who**. But even as a departure story, Clara's exit from **Doctor Who** subverts a trend among modern companion departures in which the companions are forced through exceptional and often traumatic situations to return to the more domestic lives that they fled.

For many of the modern companions, travelling with the Doctor is a defining, self-actualising moment in their lives. Rose once described it as showing her 'a better way of living your life.'[67] Donna gained

---

[65] *The Day of the Doctor.*

[66] Fullerton, Huw, 'Jenna Coleman Says a Clara **Doctor Who** Spinoff Is "Best Left in the Imagination"'.

[67] *The Parting of the Ways.*

confidence and purpose through her travels with the Doctor, at one point literally becoming the most important woman in the universe[68].

But there are also indications that life with the Doctor becomes so essential to the companions that they often can't contemplate a life without him. At one point Amy tells the Doctor: 'There was a time, there were years, when I couldn't live without you. When just the whole everyday thing would drive me crazy.'[69] Rose and Donna similarly express their desire to travel with the Doctor forever, with Donna saying, 'How could I ever go back to normal life after seeing this?'[70]

So when the 21st-century companions do eventually leave, it's rarely voluntarily – only Martha is the exception to this trend[71].

Rose is forced to leave the Doctor and return to her family no less than three separate times. On the first two occasions in *The Parting of the Ways* (2005) and *Doomsday* (2006), the Doctor forces her to leave a dangerous situation and return to her family. And both times, Rose returns to him and expresses her desire to stay with him, regardless of the danger. On the third and final time they are separated in *Journey's End*, the Doctor returns Rose and her family to a parallel universe. When Rose expresses her desire to stay with the Doctor, he rebuffs her and instead tasks her with reforming a part-human clone of himself, implying that his clone could love her and have a domestic life with her in a way that he never could.

---

[68] *Journey's End*.
[69] *The Power of Three* (2012).
[70] *The Doctor's Daughter*.
[71] *Last of the Time Lords* (2007).

Donna first met the Doctor in *Doomsday* (2006) after she was accidentally transported onto the TARDIS in the middle of her ill-fated wedding. After her travels with the Doctor in *The Runaway Bride* (2006), she's determined never to go back to the kind of life she was living before she met him. But after she absorbs all of his knowledge in a freak accident, the Doctor forcibly erases all of her memories of him and their adventures together in order to save her life. He leaves her back on Earth with her family, where she soon returns to her old way of life.

Even though Donna can't remember her adventures with the Doctor, her grandfather Wilf says that sometimes she has 'this look on her face, like she's so sad, but she can't remember why.'[72] Nevertheless, a short time later Donna marries another man. As her wedding present, the Doctor surreptitiously gives her a winning lottery ticket to ensure that she and her husband are financially well-off.

At first it seems like Amy Pond might be an exception to this rule. During series 5, there's tension between her desire to travel with the Doctor and her impending marriage to Rory Williams. That tension is made explicit in the episode *Amy's Choice* (2010), in which she is made to literally choose between two realities – one in which she's still travelling with the Doctor and one in which she's married, settled down, and expecting a child with Rory. That tension is resolved in the episode *The Big Bang* (2010) when Amy marries Rory and then brings him along to continue travelling with the Doctor immediately after their wedding. She's the woman who can have it all.

Except she can't have it forever. In their second-to-last episode, *The*

---

[72] *The End of Time.*

Power of Three (2012), Amy and Rory feel pressure to make a choice between continuing to travel with the Doctor or building their life as a married couple on Earth. In *The Angels Take Manhattan* (2012), that choice is forced on Amy. Rory is transported back in time by a Weeping Angel, and his name appears on a nearby gravestone, indicating he has lived his entire life and died in the past without Amy. Because they have created too many paradoxes in New York City, the Doctor is not able to travel back in time in the TARDIS to bring Rory back.

So Amy is forced to choose – she can either go back in time to join Rory and never see the Doctor again, or she can keep travelling with the Doctor. She chooses to let the Weeping Angel send her back in time so that she can live out the rest of her life with Rory. The Doctor later reads a note from Amy, where she says that she and Rory lived a happy life together. In an unshot scene written by Chris Chibnall and released by the BBC in storyboard form, it is revealed that Amy and Rory adopted a son during this time[73].

In his examination of gender roles in **Doctor Who**, Piers Britton examined how the companions' departure stories fit into how the show reflects and confirms heteronormativity and patriarchal authority. Britton posits that beginning with Russell T Davies' tenure as showrunner for **Doctor Who**, unresolved sexual tension became a key part of the relationship between the Doctor and the companion, which created a heteronormative imbalance between the two that put the companion at a disadvantage[74].

---

[73] '**Doctor Who**: "PS" – Series 7 2012 – BBC One'.
[74] Britton, *TARDISbound*, p117.

Britton argued that 'Davies' season-finale episodes, especially those in which companions' incumbencies ended, were key moments for the upholding of compulsory heterosexuality.'[75] Rose and Donna particularly followed this model. They found 'excitement, freedom, power and knowledge [...] via masculine patronage, in this case offered by the Doctor,' and had no choice but to leave when the Doctor forced them to 'accept the role he assigns them, usually within the bosom of the nuclear family.'[76] Donna was returned to her family and was married soon after, while Rose was given an explicit caregiving role **and** a new partner for an explicitly heterosexual relationship.

Britton doesn't include Amy within this model, arguing instead that she subverts it because of the straightforward way in which the show addresses and resolves the sexual tension between Amy and the Doctor and by the agency she displays in *The Big Bang*. However, as his book was published in 2011 and only analysed **Doctor Who** up to series 5, it's fair to note that he had an incomplete view of Amy's full story arc.

I would argue that Amy's story also reflects and confirms compulsory heteronormativity. But it doesn't follow the model Britton outlines between the Doctor, his companions, and the companions' families. Rather, it affirms compulsory heteronormativity within Amy and Rory's marriage.

During series 6 and 7, the Doctor is a constant disruptor in Amy and Rory's marriage. As a direct result of their association with the Doctor, Amy and Rory's only child is taken from them in *A Good Man*

---

[75] Britton, *TARDISbound*, p129.
[76] Britton, *TARDISbound*, p133.

Goes to War (2011), to be turned into a weapon to kill the Doctor. Due to this experience, Amy is rendered infertile. Her guilt and shame over being unable to live up to the heteronormative ideal of being able to provide Rory with children leads her to attempt to divorce him in *Asylum of the Daleks* (2012).

They reconcile, but they still aren't quite able to achieve domestic bliss. The Doctor's unpredictable intrusions into their life make it difficult for them to build a normal life on Earth. It's only after they are permanently separated from the Doctor that they're able to have a normal domestic life on Earth and finally achieve the heteronormative ideal of having children by adopting a son.

There is some debate about whether or not Amy is able to exert her own agency when she is forced to choose between returning to Rory or remaining with the Doctor in *The Angels Take Manhattan*. Technically, she does make a choice. But Britton argues that during Davies' tenure 'female protagonists were either denied agency or else their defining moments of autonomy were acts of self-sacrifice or obedience to institutional expectation.'[77] If we can say that Amy exercised her autonomy in this moment, she showed obedience to the institutional, heteronormative expectation to choose her husband over the Doctor.

Regardless, Amy isn't able to have both the fulfilling life of adventure and her marriage to Rory at the same time. In the end, the most obvious and problematic aspect of their relationship is that she is forced to chose between a fulfilling life and her marriage at all.

In the cases of Donna and Rose particularly, Una McCormack

---

[77] Britton, *TARDISbound*, p129.

described these types of departure scenarios as portraying the 'nightmare of domesticity.' The narrative tension in Donna and Rose's stories is between their fear of returning to their boring domestic lives and unsatisfactory relationships and their dream of escaping to a more exciting and fulfilling life with the Doctor. When given the choice between returning home or remaining with the Doctor, there is no question what they would choose – and they repeatedly make their preferences explicitly clear.

And yet, ultimately, neither Donna or Rose gets to make that choice. The Doctor overrules their own preferences and sends them both home. To McCormack, it is as if the show is saying that 'adventure is something you can do for awhile [...] but then – inevitably, relentlessly – the wedding day will arrive, after which it's best to put these things out of your mind, or else the pain of remembering this life without limits might kill you.'[78]

Clara is the rare companion who isn't forced back into a domestic life when she departs the show. She expressed a clear desire to travel with the Doctor regardless of the risks, and although she didn't leave entirely unscathed, she is able to set the terms of her departure and continue to live the life of excitement and adventure she so clearly craved.

Although there is significant tension between Clara's everyday domestic life and her life with the Doctor in her earlier seasons, by the beginning of series 9 there is practically no tension being drawn

[78] McCormack, Una, 'Amy's Choice: **Doctor Who** Companions and the Nightmare of Domesticity', p212. Myles, LM and Liz Barr, eds, *Companion Piece: Women Celebrate the Humans, Aliens, and Tin Dogs of Doctor Who.*

between Clara's domestic life and her life with the Doctor. She is fully committed to travelling with him. Additionally, she would find a normal life unappealing and unfulfilling. After *Hell Bent* aired, Moffat said: 'I couldn't imagine Clara going back to an ordinary life, could you? [...] She'd be obliged to become ordinary; towards the end, she's not even good at simulating that.'[79]

And yet, when the Doctor pulls Clara out of her timeline moments before her death and saves her life, he is determined to return her to a normal life with no memories of their adventures together. He proposes bringing her 'somewhere safe, somewhere out of the way.' At that moment in the narrative, when the audience does not yet know that Clara still has her memories, they might assume she's been left in a rural diner to live out the rest of her life as a waitress.

And given the Doctor's suggestion in *Under the Lake* that Clara find a new boyfriend, we might even assume he is hoping that Clara will find herself another relationship, settle down, and live a normal domestic life. He was, after all, able to return Donna and Rose to their domestic lives and assist them in setting up secure heterosexual relationships. He appears to be following the same pattern of behaviour, beginning with overruling his companion's wishes and deciding on her behalf that she should return to a normal life.

But unlike Donna and Rose, Clara's wishes are heard and respected. She leaves him with her memories intact and a TARDIS of her own, with the ability to travel throughout time and space and continue to have the adventures that she always wanted. *Hell Bent*'s narrative doesn't condemn her to the 'nightmare of domesticity' or trap her

---

[79] Cook, Benjamin, '*Heaven Sent* and *Hell Bent*'.

within compulsory heteronormativity. Clara is able to live her own life, on her own terms.

While a normal domestic life would be totally unsuitable for Clara, it's worth questioning whether the pattern established in modern companion departures problematically stigmatises the domestic sphere. All of the companions are, to some degree, attempting to escape their domestic lives. When faced with dull jobs, plodding daily routines, nagging families, and unsatisfying relationships, who wouldn't want to run off with a charming stranger to see all of time and space?

That's part of the escapist charm of **Doctor Who**. The audience can sympathise with the companion's domestic troubles and dream of leaving all of those problems behind too. And yet, there is still value in the domestic sphere, and perhaps value in showing why a companion might voluntarily want to leave the Doctor in order to return to her everyday life. As McCormack says:

> 'Whatever we may fantasise, home life – the feminine sphere – exists, supporting dilettante adventurers or career-minded young people in their endeavours, no matter how much we might try to wish it away, or pretend it isn't there. Opening up the space alongside the space where the Doctor travels could well be a radical move: recognition that adventure doesn't really take place in a vacuum or a vortex. It is dependent upon quieter, private spaces.'[80]

As affirming as it is to see Clara exercise her autonomy to avoid being trapped in an unsatisfying life, perhaps the more radical story would

---

[80] McCormack, 'Amy's Choice', p211.

have been one in which she recognised on her own that there was a valuable life to be lived outside of one with the Doctor. It would be more radical still if that choice wasn't compelled by extraordinary circumstances. Consider Martha, who still remains an exception to this trend. Unlike Amy or Clara, Martha gets to leave the Doctor without a life-threatening circumstance forcing her hand. After reflection and consideration, she seeks out the Doctor, lays out her reasons for wanting to stay on Earth, and leaves to build a new life. That amount of narrative space and autonomy is rarely afforded to a departing companion.

Still, the thought of escaping our everyday lives to travel untethered through time and space will always exert a powerful pull on our imaginations. And in this escapist fantasy, it is undeniably empowering to see a companion able to access this ability on her own, without having to rely on the shifting whims of the Doctor. Clara is truly the hero of her own narrative now, and the rest of the story is hers to write.

CHAPTER 4: MEMORIES BECOME SONG
Clara's Theme and Letimotif in *Hell Bent*

'Is it a sad song?'

[Clara]

Out in the sunbaked Nevada desert, a man wanders out the dust into a lonely diner. He has no money, but he can play the guitar slung over his shoulder. He offers a song for a lemonade. The waitress smiles and accepts – it's a fair trade. It could be the start of a fairytale, but it's not clear who would be the magician of this story. The woman says she came to this lonely outpost by magic. The man smiles, and says he travelled by magic too. And then he plays a magic trick: as he strums his guitar, the music echoes from every single speaker around them. The woman smiles, and believes him.

There's something sweet but unsettling about this interaction. These two people should know each other, and yet, they're strangers to each other. Still, the man keeps playing his guitar. The woman asks the man if he's playing a sad song. He replies: 'Nothing's sad till it's over. Then everything is.' She asks him what the song is called. He thinks that the song is called 'Clara.'

The man, of course, is the Doctor, and the woman is Clara Oswald. And the song that the Doctor is playing on his guitar is Clara's theme, originally composed by Murray Gold. It's a rare case in which a musical theme becomes diegetic – heard, played, and named by the characters within the narrative of the show. Although the theme can also be heard extradiegetically in its original form during key moments in *Hell Bent*, its transformation reflects a more complex character action. It's not simply marking key character moments;

instead, it is reflecting a process in which one character is recreating their memories of another character.

Hell Bent is not the first story in which we see the 12th Doctor playing a guitar. This particular talent of the Doctor's was suggested by actor Peter Capaldi, who is himself a talented guitarist, before series 9 began filming. His suggestion was embraced wholeheartedly, and the Doctor was given multiple scenes throughout series 9 to play the guitar. Capaldi even shopped for the Doctor's guitar himself, choosing a Yamaha guitar based on his own interpretation of what kind of guitar the Doctor would want to play[81].

One of the more iconic moments in the first episode of series 9, *The Magician's Apprentice*, saw the Doctor enter a medieval arena atop a tank, shredding out the **Doctor Who** theme tune on his new guitar. This was another example of the Doctor making theme music diegetic within the show – as if the sheer audacity of what the Doctor was about to do literally required his own theme music to be accompanying him. The use of Clara's theme in *Hell Bent*, however, was more poignant and driven by character growth.

Clara's theme was originally created for her first appearance in series 7 by series composer Murray Gold. It had a romantic, almost fairytale quality to it. The music starts off light and breathy, with the theme's distinctive notes being plucked out in a way that sounds reminiscent of a music box. Then the music gradually swells as more instruments join the accompaniment, imparting a sense of growing wonder. Chimes ring out, lending even more of a fairytale perception. The theme then alternates between lighter, breathier moments and

---

[81] Itzkoff, Dave, 'Peter Capaldi Prepares for His Final Season of **Doctor Who**'.

more grandiose moments, before ending on a deep, low note. It has a narrative quality to it – as if the music is guiding the listener through a journey.

Rather fittingly, Clara's theme was originally entitled 'Clara?'[82] At the time of her introduction, it reflected the ongoing mystery about Clara's character during series 7. By the time she's about to depart, the title could reflect Clara's status as a quasi-Doctor figure. Just as the signature question to ask in **Doctor Who** is 'Doctor who?', the Doctor finds himself asking 'Clara? Clara who?' The name itself has become a question. It could also reflect the Doctor's loss of all of his memories about Clara. She has become a mystery to him. And so the song represents a different kind of question to him – who is Clara, and why was she so important?

In *Hell Bent*, Clara's theme is used as a leitmotif to guide the audience through the Doctor's loss of those memories and his attempt to reconstruct them. The theme is heard extradiegetically in its original form at key moments when Clara impacts the Doctor.

The first time the audience hears the original theme is after the Doctor admits in the cloisters that he stayed in the confession dial for four and a half billion years in an attempt to save Clara's life. Clara interrupts him and halts his escape in order to tell him something very important. But as she is about to tell him, the camera pulls up and away, leaving them to their conversation in private. The only thing the audience can hear in that moment is Clara's theme. When the Doctor later confesses in the diner that Clara told him something very important, but that he has no memory of what she said, Clara's theme can be heard again, audibly linking the two moments

---

[82] Gold, Murray, *Doctor Who Series 7 Original Television Soundtrack*.

together.

Parts of Clara's original theme can also be heard at key moments during the confrontation between Clara and the Doctor in the TARDIS. When the Doctor finally realises that he was wrong to try to erase Clara's memories, the distinctive opening notes of her theme can be briefly heard. It can also be heard after the Doctor uses the neural block and begins to lose his memories of Clara. A slowed down version of the theme is used in this moment – as if the notes to the melody, along with the Doctor's memories of Clara, are slowly fading away.

By contrast, the diegetic use of Clara's theme as played on the guitar represents the Doctor's attempts to cope with the loss of those memories. Consider the first moment we hear the Doctor play Clara's theme. In its original form, Clara's theme is uplifting and optimistic. But the Doctor plays it haltingly, as if he's trying to remember the tune. The Doctor's electric guitar creates a harsher sound, and without the twinkling piano or chimes, Clara's theme loses some of its more magical qualities. It has an almost mournful sound, prompting Clara to ask if it is a sad song. And it is – because the Doctor is grieving her, even as he is still struggling to understand the scale of what he has lost.

The transformation itself also reflects his process of reconstructing an impression of who Clara is. The Doctor tells Clara that 'memories become stories' when they are forgotten. Clara suggests that 'maybe some of them become songs.' This suggests that Clara's theme as played by the Doctor is a reconstruction of the Doctor's memories. It's not an exact replica of the original theme because, of course, his own original memories have been taken from him. The process of transforming the song reflects the altering and reconstruction of his memories.

Extradiegetically, Clara's theme is a leitmotif which cues the audience that an important character moment for her is about to occur. Intradiegetically, the Doctor's rendition of that theme provides his own internal narrative cues about who Clara was and why she was so important to him. Transforming her theme is his own creative act of putting Clara back into the narrative of his life after she was erased from it.

Of course, Clara was with him in the diner the whole time, even if he didn't know it. For the most part, she lets him tell his story uninterrupted, but she does nudge him occasionally to view the story in a different way. It is she, after all, who tells the Doctor that the song he is playing might be a memory of the important thing she told him in the cloisters. She is guiding the recreation of the Doctor's memories, and in turn rebuilding her own narrative within **Doctor Who**.

After all, she's the star of her own show, the lead character in "Clara Who". And her fairytale isn't over – it's just beginning. But she has one more magic trick to play. True to her earlier claim that she arrived by magic, she steps back into the control room of her own TARDIS and vanishes into thin air. As the walls of the diner dissolve around him, the Doctor keeps playing her song on his guitar, as if the audacity of what she is about to do requires her to be accompanied by her own theme tune.

CHAPTER 5: HERE COMES THE GENERAL

Setting the Stage for Jodie Whittaker

'Dear Lord, how do you cope with all that ego?'

[The General]

On Christmas Day 2017, 54 years after **Doctor Who**'s first episode premiered and after 15 men[83] had portrayed the titular character, the 12th Doctor regenerated into the 13th, and Jodie Whittaker became the first woman to portray the Doctor[84]. It was a historic moment decades in the making.

In the reckoning of this regeneration, Steven Moffat will have a complicated legacy. He consistently expressed support for a woman to eventually be cast as the Doctor. But despite having three opportunities to do so, he never cast a woman in the role. And his advocacy was often undermined by his own statements about why he never cast a woman, and his own unfortunately glib humour.

And yet, Moffat has also been responsible for laying the groundwork within the show for the Doctor to eventually regenerate into a woman. Since his very first moments as showrunner, he has written lines and created characters on **Doctor Who** to establish the continuity that Time Lords could change their gender when they

---

[83] William Hartnell, Patrick Troughton, Jon Pertwee, Tom Baker, Peter Davison, Colin Baker, Sylvester McCoy, Paul McGann, Christopher Eccleston, David Tennant, Matt Smith, and Peter Capaldi originally played the 12 numbered Doctors. John Hurt portrayed the War Doctor. Richard Hurndall and David Bradley played the first Doctor after Hartnell's death.

[84] *Twice Upon a Time* (2017).

regenerate. As part of that campaign, Moffat argues that he was able to normalise the idea and generate audience support and demand for a woman portraying the iconic role. His campaign culminated in *Hell Bent* with the General's regeneration from a white man to a black woman. That regeneration served as a final, unavoidable, non-negotiable statement that such regenerations were normal and possible. And, Moffat hoped, it would increase calls for a woman to eventually portray the role.

The idea that a woman could one day portray the Doctor has a long and fraught history. It came up multiple times in multiple mediums, but was rarely considered seriously, or without a parodic or heavily stigmatised approach. The first prominent mention of the idea was in the press conference announcing Tom Baker's departure from the role, when Baker said that he wished the next Doctor the very best of luck, '**whoever he or she is**'[85].

However, as producer John Nathan-Turner later recounted, Baker's comment was only intended as a joke between the two of them at the expense of the journalists at the press conference. Baker's comment generated plenty of press coverage and interest in who his successor might be, which Nathan Turner certainly appreciated. But Nathan Turner regarded the whole idea as being fairly ridiculous, writing a few years after the press conference that 'There was never a chance **then** – nor do I think there ever will be – that the Doctor could be played by a woman. Absolutely not!'[86]

Nevertheless, the idea persisted. Sydney Newman, the former Head

---

[85] Haining, Peter, ed, *Doctor Who: A Celebration*, p163 (emphasis in original).
[86] Haining, *A Celebration*, p163.

of Drama at the BBC and one of **Doctor Who**'s original creators, proposed having the Doctor become a woman only a few years later. The latter half of the 1980s were a perilous time for **Doctor Who**. The show had been briefly cancelled in 1985, before receiving a reprieve and being put on an extended hiatus. In 1986, BBC One controller Michael Grade reached out to Newman to discuss the show's future. A month after their first meeting, Newman sent Grade his proposal to save the show.

Newman had two radical ideas about what to do with the Doctor's character. First, he proposed that the second Doctor, Patrick Troughton, briefly return to the role. Then, the Doctor should be 'metamorphosed' into a woman. It was a provocative idea, but Newman seemed determined that the idea shouldn't be viewed as a gimmick. He wrote that the idea

> 'requires some considerable thought – mainly because I want to avoid a flashy Hollywood "Wonder Woman" because this kind of hero[ine] has no flaws – and a character with no flaws is a bore.'[87]

Newman wrote that if he was given more time, he could create this new woman Doctor. However, there is no record of how – or even if – Grade ever responded to Newman's proposal, and Newman's ideas never came off the page.

Doctor Who was cancelled in 1989 after eight men had played the Doctor. It briefly returned in a 1996 film with Paul McGann cast in the leading role, but the movie failed to revive the franchise. But **Doctor Who** lived on through other mediums, and so did the idea of

---

[87] Newman Sydney, and Graeme Burk, *Head of Drama*, p518.

making the Doctor a woman.

The first time a woman portrayed the Doctor in an officially licensed production was in the 1999 Comic Relief Special *The Curse of Fatal Death*, written by future showrunner Steven Moffat. This parody sent up many of the tropes associated with **Doctor Who**, including regeneration. At the very end of the special, the Doctor regenerated rapidly from one celebrity to another, before finally regenerating into a woman, played by Joanna Lumley. Each celebrity regeneration was comedic in its own way, but Lumley's version of the Doctor is parodied in a way that relies heavily on her gender. There's a joke about her breasts, and the Sonic Screwdriver is used in a visual gag implying she could use it as a vibrator ('It has **three** settings!'[88]). And now that the Doctor was being portrayed by a woman, homosexual subtexts that had existed between the Doctor and the Master for decades were made explicit and heterosexual. The Doctor and the Master suddenly realise that they find each other attractive, and as the episode closes, they walk off together with the Doctor's hand firmly on the Master's backside.

The next time we saw a woman portray the Doctor in an officially licensed production was in the 2003 Big Finish audio play *Exile*, a part of the **Unbound** series which proposed hypothetical 'What if...?' scenarios unbound by the series' continuity. *Exile* asked what might have happened if the second Doctor had escaped the Time Lords at the end of *The War Games* (1969) – and in this alternate scenario, the second Doctor regenerates into a woman.

However, the idea that the Doctor could regenerate into a woman was highly stigmatised. The Doctor in *Exile* could only be a woman,

---

[88] *The Curse of Fatal Death*.

the audience is told, because the only time Time Lords change their gender during regeneration is if they commit suicide. Every other Time Lord who appears in this story treats this type of regeneration as a shameful, embarrassing thing. And the female Doctor, so upset and depressed at being forced to hide herself on Earth, is driven to repeated excessive drinking [89]. Nicholas Briggs, the executive producer for Big Finish who also wrote *Exile*, later expressed his regret about the story after Jodie Whittaker was cast as the Doctor. He intended this Doctor to be an atypical Doctor, chaotic and comedic, but admitted that a 'lot of bad decisions' were made on that story.

Although neither *The Curse of Fatal Death* or *Exile* were part of the show's official continuity, neither of these stories portrayed a woman Doctor in a particularly positive light. And neither generated much enthusiasm or support for a woman to portray the Doctor. Briggs himself said that if they had done a better job with their interpretation of a woman Doctor, they might have been able to write further Big Finish audios for her, as they did with some of the other actors who portrayed alternate Doctors in the **Unbound** series[90].

When **Doctor Who** came back in 2005, the new production team never considered casting a woman as the Doctor. After Jodie Whittaker's casting was announced, showrunner Russell T Davies said he would have loved to cast a woman as the Doctor, but that 'it wasn't on the to-do list back in 2005 as we were busy getting the

---

[89] Briggs, Nicholas, *Exile*.
[90] Kibble-White, Graham, 'The XIII Chromosome'. DWM #516.

programme up and running in the first place.'[91] His comments suggest that not casting a woman as the Doctor was both an oversight and an impossibility – that even had they thought of doing it, it might have interfered with their ability to successfully relaunch the show. After Christopher Eccleston left the show later that year, David Tennant was cast as the Doctor. He remained in the role until the end of 2009, when Davies also stepped down as showrunner.

When Tennant announced he was leaving the role, there was some minor speculation about whether a woman would take over as the Doctor. Rather oddly, Catherine Tate and Catherine Zeta Jones were both suggested as potential replacements[92]. Davies himself even suggested that Lesley Sharp, Judi Dench, or Amy Winehouse would be interesting in the role. However, in the same interview, Davies also said that Tennant's replacement should not be a woman. Although he felt that children would not have a problem with seeing a woman in the role, he imagined that fathers would have a serious problem with the idea because 'they will then imagine they will have to describe sex changes to their children.'[93] This suggests that Davies saw existing social stigma as the major barrier against a woman Doctor at the time.

Years later, Moffat simply stated that he believed it was 'too early'[94] to cast a woman as the Doctor after Tennant stepped down. Matt Smith, a relatively unknown actor at the time, eventually got the role. Although Moffat didn't cast a woman as the Doctor when he

[91] 'Russell T Davies: I Wish I Had Cast a Woman as Dr Who'.
[92] Davies, Caroline and David Smith, 'Dr Who? Big Names Lose Out to Matt Smith'.
[93] Dowell, Ben, '"Amy Winehouse Would Be a Great Doctor"'.
[94] Moffat, Steven, 'Steven Moffat On...'. DWM #494.

took over as showrunner, he did begin laying the groundwork for a woman to eventually portray the lead role.

Moffat's approach focused primarily on establishing the continuity within **Doctor Who** that Time Lords could change their gender when they regenerate. He also wanted to normalise the idea that a woman could play the Doctor. When asked how he prepared the way for Whittaker's casting, he said that one of his worries was having '*Daily Mail*-reading viewers saying, "That's not the same person!"'[95] His approach, therefore, was designed to move those audiences step-by-step towards accepting a woman as the Doctor[96].

Moffat's campaign began in his very first moments as showrunner, during the post-regeneration scene written by him for *The End of Time*. As the 11th Doctor examines his brand new body, he notices his slightly longer hair and yells in disbelief, '*I'm a girl!*'[97] After checking his Adam's apple he comes to the conclusion that he is not, in fact, a girl. But the idea had been suggested explicitly within the show for the first time that one day, perhaps, the Doctor could be.

The next time the idea emerged was in *The Doctor's Wife* (2011), an episode penned by Neil Gaiman. The Doctor receives a message with the image of a snake eating its own tail stamped on it, indicating it's from a fellow Time Lord known as the Corsair. The image represents a tattoo the Corsair had in every regeneration. As the Doctor tells Amy and Rory, The Corsair 'didn't feel like himself unless he had the

---

[95] Mulkern, Patrick, 'Time Gentlemen'. *Radio Times*, 9 to 15 December 2017.

[96] Setchfield, Nick, 'Time for Goodbye'. *SFX* #295, January 2018.

[97] *The End of Time*.

tattoo. Or herself, a couple of times.'[98] The Corsair became the first known Time Lord to have changed their gender during regeneration. Although the line was originally written by Gaiman, Moffat approved of its inclusion and expanded on the characterisation of the female regeneration of the Corsair, adding the very Moffat-esque description that she was 'a bad girl.'[99]

The idea was referenced again in 'The Night of the Doctor' (2013), a short mini-episode released before the 50th anniversary special episode. At the end of *The Name of the Doctor* (2013) it was revealed that there was an previously unknown regeneration of the Doctor between the eighth and ninth Doctors, who would be portrayed in the anniversary special by John Hurt. 'The Night of the Doctor' served as a prequel to show how the eighth Doctor regenerated into the War Doctor. After his near-death on Karn, the Doctor is offered an elixir by the Sisterhood of Karn to trigger his regeneration. The Sisterhood's elixir would allow him to choose his next regeneration, and the Doctor is offered a variety of options, including the ability to choose whether he would be a man or a woman[100]. Ultimately, he decides he wants to be a 'warrior,' and regenerates into a man again.

'The Night of the Doctor' reveals one of the fundamental contradictions at the heart of Moffat's continuity strategy. The decision to create a previously unknown regeneration of the Doctor between the eighth and ninth Doctors was driven largely by production needs. Christopher Eccleston had decided not to reappear in the 50th anniversary special, and Moffat needed to

[98] *The Doctor's Wife*.
[99] Gaiman, Neil, Tumblr post, 28 July 2017.
[100] 'The Night of the Doctor'.

present a 'big idea' to the BBC for the episode. So instead of featuring Eccleston's Doctor, Moffat decided to create a new Doctor that no one had known about – specifically one that would be played by 'the most famous actor in the world' who 'might have been cast as the Doctor during the long hiatus.'[101] Moffat immediately thought of John Hurt for the role, and Hurt was cast almost immediately. So although Moffat had created an entirely new Doctor, with a new opportunity to cast a woman in the role, he did not use that opportunity to cast a woman.

It should be noted that the War Doctor would not have been the ideal regeneration to introduce an actor who was not a white male into the role. The War Doctor was a fallen Doctor. The Doctor's later regenerations treated the War Doctor as a shameful secret, and even the War Doctor was adamant that he did not deserve the name 'the Doctor' because he had fallen so far from the Doctor's ideals. Similarly to *Exile*, having the War Doctor be the first woman Doctor would have unintentionally brought even more stigma to the idea that the Doctor could regenerate into a woman. And yet, even as 'The Night of the Doctor' continued to reinforce the idea that the Doctor could one day regenerate into a woman, it continued the tradition of only presenting white men in the role.

Between *The Name of the Doctor* and 'The Night of the Doctor', another casting controversy was unfolding. Smith announced that he would be stepping down from the title role in June 2013, sending

---

[101] Mulkern, Patrick, 'Steven Moffat Finally Reveals Why John Hurt Replaced Christopher Eccleston in the Doctor Who 50th Anniversary Special'.

speculation and debate about whether a woman could be the next Doctor to a new pitch. A flurry of thinkpieces were published online debating back and forth whether the next Doctor should be a woman[102]. *The Sunday Times* reported that 'informed sources'[103] at the BBC were suggesting that a woman would be cast.

Various women were speculated to be in the running for the role, notably Olivia Coleman and Helen Mirren. When Ladbrokes released their odds on who would be the next Doctor, Coleman was one of the leading contenders, leading her to joke that she wouldn't put any money on it'[104]. Mirren flatly denied she would be taking the role, but strongly supported a woman playing the Doctor, saying that 'a gay, black female Doctor Who would be best of all.'[105]

Even the BBC encouraged speculation that the next Doctor would be a woman. The official BBC website ran a poll asking fans who they thought would be the next Doctor with four options; those options included a female actor who had appeared in the show and a female actor who hadn't appeared in the show. And the official announcement of the special programme that would announce

[102] Helmuth, Laura, 'The Next Doctor Should Be a Woman. You Should Care Even if You Don't Watch Doctor Who.'

[103] Brooks, Richard, 'Sexterminate! Doctor Who May Come Back as a Woman'.

[104] Galton, Susanna, '**Broadchurch** Star Olivia Colman Jokes that **Doctor Who** Fans Shouldn't Bet Any Money on Her Taking Over from Matt Smith'.

[105] Daly, Emma, 'Dame Helen Mirren: "A Gay, Black Female Doctor Who Would Be the Best of All"'.

Peter Capaldi's casting was kept carefully gender-neutral[106].

But the speculation soon began to sour. The day before the announcement was made, bookmaker William Hill suspended betting on Capaldi as he suddenly became the runaway favourite for the role[107]. The day of the announcement, celebrity photographer Rankin inadvertently revealed the next Doctor would be a man after tweeting that he'd just photographed the new actor[108].

Even as it became clearer that the next Doctor was not going to be a woman, the special programme announcing Capaldi's casting went to absurd lengths to fuel last-minute speculation that the next Doctor might be a woman. At the beginning of the programme, an interview with Smith was shown in which he discussed his relationship with the next Doctor. Smith carefully avoided saying Capaldi's name, but repeatedly used male pronouns to refer to him. After the interview aired, programme host Zoe Ball immediately acknowledged that Smith had used male pronouns but attempted to deflect, saying that it 'could be awkward if the next Doctor turns out to be a woman! It could happen, it might happen one day, you never know!'

It was likely that her deflection was an attempt to accommodate pre-recorded interviews that were about to air. But it was awkward and confusing in context. Smith's interview had included personal anecdotes about interacting with Capaldi to show how long he'd

[106] Kissell, Ted B, 'The Depressing, Disappointing Maleness of **Doctor Who**'s New Time Lord'.

[107] Westbrook, Caroline, 'Betting Ends on **Dr Who** as Peter Capaldi's Odds Shorten'.

[108] Rankin, tweet posted 1:47pm GMT, 4 August 2013.

known and been friendly with his successor. So for Ball's statement to be true, Smith would have had to have been deliberately lying in order to spring a surprise reveal about the next Doctor's gender. Ball's statement appeared to be an over-the-top and disingenuous attempt to generate last-minute enthusiasm that a woman could be the next Doctor.

In the next round of pre-recorded interviews, groups of celebrities and actors discussed what they would like to see in the next Doctor. Stephen Hawking said that 'it would be amazing if the next Doctor was a woman.' A portion of Moffat's interview was shown in response, in which he said that he had established in **Doctor Who** that it could happen, but refused to say whether or not the next Doctor would be a woman. And then, without any apparent prompting at all, he went on to add:

> 'I like that Helen Mirren has been saying that we should have a female Doctor. I would like to go on record, I think it's time that the Queen was played by a man.'[109]

The comment prompted an immediate backlash. The joke was apparently meant to imply that Helen Mirren was hogging the role of Queen Elizabeth II. She had portrayed the Queen twice, first in the 2006 film *The Queen* and then in the play *The Audience*, which had premiered in the West End earlier that year. So why not let another person – even a man! – have a go.

And yet, the two situations were so radically different that it was an obviously false equivalence. Helen Mirren was portraying a real, living, prominent figure. She had portrayed the Queen in two

---

[109] *Doctor Who Live: The Next Doctor.*

separate productions seven years apart. The Doctor had been portrayed by multiple men since **Doctor Who** first premiered nearly 50 years earlier. And most importantly, the Doctor was a fictional character who, by the very rules Moffat had helped establish, could also be portrayed by a woman.

Commentator Ryan McGee also noted that the optics of the comment within the overall programme were wounding to many fans who had been hoping that a woman could be the next Doctor. Moffat could've simply ended his statement after noting that the rules of the show allowed a woman to one day portray the Doctor. Instead, he singled out Helen Mirren, who was at that point one of the most prominent actresses who had been saying that a woman should one day be given the role. And the interview was shown to a live, in-house audience, whose laughter could be heard over the comment. In context, it felt as if Moffat and the BBC were setting up the very idea of a woman portraying the Doctor as ridiculous and amusing[110]. That was how I interpreted it at the time. I wrote immediately afterward on my blog that I felt 'a huge, aching sense of disappointment with Moffat,'[111] a response which was quoted or linked to by the *Rolling Stone*[112] and the *Washington Post*[113] as an illustration of broader fan outrage against Moffat's joke.

Moffat would then spend the next weeks and months explaining why

---

[110] McGee, Ryan, '**Doctor Who**: Peter Capaldi Can Stay but Steven Moffat Needs to Go'.

[111] Franke, Alyssa, Whovian Feminism Tumblr post, 4 August 2013.

[112] Holslin, Peter, 'Forget Peter Capaldi: It's Time for a Female on **Dr Who**'

[113] Reese, Diana, 'The TARDIS: No Girls Allowed as the Doctor'.

he didn't choose a woman to be the 12th Doctor and what would need to happen for a woman to be cast in the role. The one essential point Moffat emphasised was that Peter Capaldi was the only person he ever considered for the role[114]. He also repeatedly emphasised that it was possible within the narrative of **Doctor Who** for the Doctor to one day regenerate into a woman. But when he expounded on why, specifically, he didn't choose a woman for the 12th Doctor, he offered varying and occasionally contradictory answers.

Immediately after the announcement that Capaldi had been cast, Moffat argued that the time simply wasn't right for a female Doctor because a large enough percentage of the audience didn't support the idea, adding that 'Oddly enough most people who said they were dead against it – and I know I'll get into trouble for saying this – were women.'[115] Although this may have reflected Moffat's anecdotal experiences at the time, polling of the British public revealed that audiences were almost evenly split about whether or not the next Doctor should be a woman, with more women than men saying that the 12th Doctor did not need to be a man.[116] He later said that he might have been able to cast a woman for the 12th Doctor, if he hadn't become 'obsessed'[117] with casting Capaldi.

At the Hay Festival 10 months later, he then argued that the decision

---

[114] Jeffery, Morgan, 'Steven Moffat on Casting Peter Capaldi: "The Doctor Was in the Room"'.

[115] Jeffery, Morgan, 'Steven Moffat on Female **Doctor Who** Rumours: "It Didn't Feel Right"'.

[116] Dahlgreen, Will, 'Doctor Who Must Be a Man'.

[117] Mulkern, Patrick, 'Time Gentlemen'.

to cast a woman as the Doctor should never be a 'political' decision. He argued that when a woman Doctor is cast, it will happen exactly the way he cast Capaldi to be the 12th Doctor – when the showrunner sits down and the perfect person for the role simply pops into their head. He said the showrunner should never 'cast for any other reason than for passion and for aesthetics. It's not a political decision, it's an aesthetic decision and will always be.'[118]

The comment is an interesting one, especially since it can be argued that continuing to cast a white male as the Doctor is itself a political decision that reinforces a status quo that privileges white men for the role. And while there were obviously arguments being made for a woman Doctor that were overtly political in tone, there were also many that were grounded in the narrative and aesthetics of the show. The *Washington Post* asked why the Doctor continued to regenerate into a white man when it seemed to have 'no lack of imagination when it comes to other characters and situations.'[119] The *Rolling Stone* said 'it's hardly a stretch to imagine the Doctor as a woman [or] person of colour'[120].

Ironically, Moffat's own words explaining the aesthetics of why he chose Capaldi as the Doctor provide a useful framework for understanding why many found Capaldi's casting to be a curious aesthetic choice. Explaining why he had chosen an older actor, Moffat said:

---

[118] Singh, Anita, 'A Female Doctor Who? Not If Politics Has Anything to Do With It'.
[119] Reese, Diana, 'The TARDIS.
[120] Holslin, 'Forget Peter Capaldi'.

'Can you imagine if we had cast another handsome yet quirky young man with entertaining hair? The show would just have become that little bit more ordinary. You start to work out what the joke is and it's never quite as magic again.'[121]

If you shorten 'handsome yet quirky young man with entertaining hair' to just 'white man,' you have the essential argument that many were making for someone other than a white man to portray the Doctor.

But Moffat would later walk back from his argument that you must cast without deliberate intent for a character's gender in a big way. In 2014, he reintroduced the iconic Time Lord the Master, played for the first time in the character's 43-year history by a woman, Michelle Gomez. And he decided to make the Master a woman long before he decided to cast Gomez.

When he recounted this casting decision later on, he admitted that approach was contradictory to his previous statements about casting, saying:

'That's exactly the kind of gimmick I'm always saying you shouldn't do, so what does it mean? I've always said in the past we cast the person, you cast an individual, you don't cast a gender, that's bananas – as [Missy] would say.'[122]

By chance he saw Michelle Gomez's name on a list of actresses being considered for another role, and decided that she would be perfect for the Master. He emphasised that, ultimately, what mattered and what sold the idea is that they found an actress who could deliver

[121] Singh, 'A Female Doctor Who?'.
[122] Mellor, Louisa, '**Doctor Who**: Steven Moffat on Series 8, Missy'.

the best performance.

But he was willing to go against his own advice for an arguably political reason – to continue his own campaign to establish the continuity that Time Lords could change their gender when they regenerate. He later stated that the reason he had decided to cast a woman as the Master was to 'once and for all absolutely establish in plain sight, so not any doubt about this whatsoever: yes, Time Lords can do **that**.'[123] In his view, it reinforced the narrative that he had been building that one day the Doctor could regenerate into a woman, too.

The culmination of Moffat's campaign comes in *Hell Bent*. The Time Lord known as the General, previously portrayed by Ken Bones in *The Day of the Doctor*[124], confronts the Doctor as he attempts to rescue Clara. The Doctor shoots him, triggering the General's regeneration. And then, for the first time onscreen, a white male Time Lord regenerated into a black woman, portrayed by actress T'nia Miller. If Missy's regeneration was intended to absolutely establish in plain sight that Time Lords could change their gender during regeneration, the General's regeneration was like a flashing neon sign.

It also normalised the regeneration of a Time Lord from a man into a woman in a critical way. Unlike the precedent set in *Exile*, the General's regeneration was not stigmatised. The General regenerated as a result of being shot – a (relatively speaking) normal way for Time Lords to regenerate, and without any of the stigma

---

[123] Kelsh, Sami, '**Doctor Who** writer Steven Moffat on Missy, the Rani and Killing Characters'.

[124] And arguably *The Time of the Doctor* (2013), where Bones provides the voice of an unnamed and unseen Time Lord.

associated with committing suicide. The General's regeneration was also treated as a largely unremarkable event by his/her fellow Time Lords. After her regeneration, a fellow soldier initially referred to the General as 'Sir' but, upon recognising that the General was now a woman, corrected himself and called her 'Ma'am.' But otherwise, he showed no concern or confusion regarding her gender.

The General, for her part, was largely unperturbed by her regeneration. In a clever twist, she revealed that the only time she had ever been a man was in her previous regeneration, and that she regarded being a woman as being 'back to normal.' So although from the audience's perspective the General's regeneration was a new and exciting departure from the expected, within the show's narrative it was a normal and expected possibility during regeneration.

The General only makes one comment regarding her/his past male regeneration: 'Dear lord, how do you cope with all that ego?' There was a small amount of backlash at the time of this episode's airing from some who claimed that the General's comment was a sexist attack on men and masculinity — as if we couldn't have a male Time Lord regenerate into a woman without putting down men as a whole. This reaction was understandable to some degree, but it ignores the larger context of the episode.

The General serves two presidents of Gallifrey during his previous regeneration in *Hell Bent*: Rassilon and the Doctor. The first walked around announcing himself as 'Rassilon the Resurrected' and thought he could trap the Doctor in his own confession dial, torture information about the Hybrid out of him, and then kill him and get away with it. The second was referred to as 'The Man Who Won the

Time War', wouldn't come out of his bedroom unless Rassilon himself marched out to the Drylands to see him, deposed the President and the High Council, shot the General, and then thought he could alter a fixed moment of time without any repercussions.

Both Rassilon and the Doctor are presented as flawed characters who are driven by their egos, and ultimately fall because they don't anticipate the consequences of their actions. These details aren't incidental to the plot — they are a core part of *Hell Bent*'s examination and critique of patriarchal impulses and toxic expressions of masculinity. The General's comment is not a general commentary about male Time Lords regenerating into women, it is a pointed critique of the particular male Time Lords who are making the General's life difficult at the moment.

Although T'nia Miller delivers a performance that is distinctly her own, the General's motivations and characterization largely remain the same following her regeneration. Once she recovers, she continues on her mission to find Clara and return her to the moment of her death. The General still remains sympathetic to both Clara and the Doctor, just as her previous regeneration was, but she will not allow them to unravel time and put billions of lives at risk. If her characterization has any implications for Jodie Whittaker's Doctor, it may be that the General remains the General no matter the gender of the actor, just as the Doctor will always remain the Doctor.

Moffat crafted the General's scene with an intentional regard for both the narrative within **Doctor Who** and the public narrative about the potential for a woman Doctor. As part of his campaign to establish the continuity for a woman to portray the Doctor, he felt it was important that none of the other characters 'make a fuss' about the General changing gender. Just like when the Master changed gender, the Doctor 'doesn't seem to regard it as of any consequence at all. Hoorah!' That nonchalance was also important for the public conversation about the Doctor becoming a woman. Moffat intended this moment to move the conversation beyond **Doctor Who** fans and into the general audience, saying that the General's on-screen regeneration would raise the issue properly 'because it's now been done prominently, with nobody making a fuss about it.'[125]

However, the decision to cast a woman Doctor wouldn't be Moffat's to make. In January 2016, Moffat announced he would be stepping down as showrunner after series 10. Nearly a year later, Capaldi announced that he would also be stepping down from the lead role after series 10. Chris Chibnall was tapped as the next showrunner, and in July 2017, Jodie Whittaker was announced as the next Doctor.

It's difficult to evaluate the success of Moffat's strategy to increase public support for a woman eventually portraying the Doctor. There is unfortunately no consistent polling on the topic, but YouGov conducted a few surveys of the British public that show evolving public attitudes towards a woman portraying the Doctor during Moffat's tenure. The surveys shouldn't be directly compared to each other, as different questions were asked each time within an entirely different context, but their results are informative.

In June of 2013, YouGov asked which characteristics that respondents thought were important for the 12th Doctor. 52% of respondents said it was important that the Doctor be a man[126]. In April of 2016, after both the Master and the General were portrayed

[125] Moffat, 'Steven Moffat on...'. DWM #494.
[126] Dahlgreen, 'Doctor Who Must Be a Man'.

by women, YouGov asked a new survey audience how they would feel about the Doctor being played by a woman. 36% of the respondents felt positively towards the idea, 25% reacted negatively, and 32% of the respondents were neutral[127]. In 2017, after Jodie Whittaker was announced as the next Doctor, YouGov asked a new audience if having a woman play the Doctor was a positive or negative move. 36% of respondents felt it was a positive move, 14% felt it was a negative move, and 43% said it was neither[128].

Again, the varying nature of the surveys mean that no definitive conclusions can be drawn from this data, but it would appear that over time, fewer people reacted negatively towards the idea of a woman playing the Doctor.

There were other outside factors that might have influenced that shift in public opinion. While the Doctor remained resolutely male, other franchises were beginning to make big and highly controversial shifts towards female protagonists. *Star Wars: The Force Awakens* (2015) brought the *Star Wars* franchise back to the big screen with a diverse cast and a woman portraying the lead protagonist. *Ghostbusters* (2016) rebooted the classic 80s franchise, this time with an all-woman rather than an all-man ensemble cast. Both films were accused of 'shoehorn[ing] in a PC ideology'[129] and putting 'minorities and women incessantly and ridiculously in your face to

---

[127] Hashimoto, Mizuho, 'Public Ready for a Black Doctor Who'.
[128] 'Do You Think Public Sector Workers Are Paid Better Than Private Sector Workers? Plus, Making the First Move and **Dr Who** Results'.
[129] Sims, David, 'The Ongoing Outcry Against the Ghostbusters Remake'.

make a **political point**[130] [emphasis in original] because of their choices to cast women in lead roles that had previously been held by men.

It's possible that by bearing the brunt of the early controversies around similar casting decisions, franchises like *Star Wars* and *Ghostbusters* helped pave the way for **Doctor Who**. Conversations about those casting controversies, and the eventual success of those films, may have shifted public opinion.

But it could be argued that there was something unique about the conversation surrounding **Doctor Who** that made the public more likely to support a woman as the Doctor. In the YouGov survey from 2016, they also asked their sampling of British citizens if they supported a woman portraying Hamlet, Sherlock Holmes, Robin Hood, or James Bond. Unlike the results for **Doctor Who**, the public was overwhelmingly negative towards a woman portraying those iconic roles[131]. YouGov didn't probe those responses further, and it would be impossible now to determine what influenced those opinions in 2016. But it's possible that explicit support from influential individuals on **Doctor Who**'s production team, such as Moffat, and the narrative within the show that a woman could be the Doctor resulted in the unique support for a woman portraying the Doctor.

Even still, there was a backlash to Whittaker's casting. The conservative, *Daily Mail*-reading viewers that Moffat was worried

---

[130] Brown, David G, 'Why *Star Wars: The Force Awakens* is a Social Justice Propaganda Film'.
[131] Hashimoto, 'Public ready for a black Doctor Who'.

about? Some of them still refused to accept the idea that a woman could portray the Doctor[132]. And the *Daily Mail* did what the *Daily Mail* was probably always going to do with any actress who would have been cast as the Doctor – they published screenshots of Whittaker from nude scenes in her previous on-screen work[133].

In the end, the only decision that mattered was Chibnall's. And according to him, he 'always knew [he] wanted the 13th Doctor to be a woman'[134]. Perhaps that was a personal choice he always intended to make. Perhaps he felt that the public demand was so insistent that he had no choice but to do it. Perhaps he felt that public support was so high that it would be the best possible choice to ensure the continuing success of **Doctor Who**. It's possible that Whittaker might have been cast as the Doctor regardless of Moffat's actions.

But when Moffat could have done nothing, he chose to proactively establish the continuity within **Doctor Who** that Time Lords could change their gender after regeneration, and repeatedly showed male Time Lords regenerating into women. And the General will be remembered as the culmination of Moffat's effort to pave the way for Jodie Whittaker.

---

[132] Duff, Seamus, 'BBC Face Furious Sexist Backlash After Announcing Jodie Whittaker as First Female Doctor Who'.
[133] Ruddick, Graham, '*Sun* and *Mail Online* Under Fire Over Nude Jodie Whittaker Pictures'.
[134] 'Jodie Whittaker: **Doctor Who**'s 13th Time Lord to Be a Woman'.

BIBLIOGRAPHY

Books

Britton, Piers D, *TARDISbound: Navigating the Universes of Doctor Who*. London, IB Tauris & Co Ltd, 2011. ISBN 9781845119256.

Buscombe, Edward, ed, *The BFI Companion to the Western*. New York, Macmillan Publishing Company, 1988. ISBN 9780689119620.

Haining, Peter, *Doctor Who: A Celebration*. London, WH Allen & Co Ltd, 1983. ISBN 9780491033510.

Harmes, Marcus K, *Doctor Who and the Art of Adaptation: 50 Years of Storytelling*. Lanham MD, Rowman & Littlefield, 2014. ISBN 9781442232853.

Myles, LM and Liz Barr, eds, *Companion Piece: Women Celebrate the Humans, Aliens, and Tin Dogs of Doctor Who*. Des Moines, Mad Norwegian Press, 2015. ISBN 9781935234197.

> McCormack, Una, 'Amy's Choice: Doctor Who Companions and the Nightmare of Domesticity'.

Newman, Sydney, and Graeme Burk, *Head of Drama*. Toronto, ECW Press, 2017. ISBN 9781770413047.

Rosa, Joseph G, *The Gunfighter: Man or Myth?* Norman OK, University of Oklahoma Press, 1960. ISBN 0806115610.

Periodicals

Doctor Who Magazine (DWM). Marvel UK, Panini, BBC, 1979-.

> Cook, Benjamin, '*Heaven Sent* and *Hell Bent*'. DWM #493, cover date Winter 2015/2016.

Cook, Benjamin, 'Heaven and Hell'. DWM #494, cover date January 2016.

Cook, Benjamin, 'The Doctor and Me'. DWM #494, cover date January 2016.

Cook, Benjamin, 'The DWM Interview'. DWM #500, cover date July 2016.

Kibble-White, Graham, 'The XIII Chromosome'. DWM #516, cover date October 2017.

Moffat, Steven, 'Steven Moffat On...'. DWM #494, cover date January 2016.

Moffat, Steven, 'Ask Steven Moffat'. DWM #504, cover date November 2016.

Mulkern, Patrick, 'Time Gentlemen'. *Radio Times*, 9 to 15 December 2017.

Setchfield, Nick, 'Time for Goodbye'. *SFX* #295, January 2018.

Television

Doctor Who Live: The Next Doctor. BBC, 2013.

Film

Stevens, George, dir, *Shane*. Paramount Pictures, 1953.

Leone, Sergio, dir, *A Fistful of Dollars*. MGM, 1967

Leone, Sergio, dir, *Once Upon A Time in the West*. Paramount Pictures, 1968.

Audio CD

Briggs, Nicholas, *Exile*. **Doctor Who: Unbound**. Big Finish Productions, 2003.

Gold, Murray, *Doctor Who Series 7 Original Television Soundtrack*. Silva Screen Records, 2013.

Web

'AFI's 10 Top 10 — Top 10 Western'. *American Film Institute,* 2016. http://www.afi.com/10top10/category.aspx?cat=3. Accessed 28 November 2017.

'*The Curse of Fatal Death* – Comic Relief Special – **Doctor Who** – BBC'. Doctor Who YouTube. 24 March 2017. https://www.youtube.com/watch?v=tp_Fw5oDMao. Accessed 10 December 2017.

'The Doctor the Ultimate Hero: Steven Moffat on the *Eleventh Hour* Panel – **Doctor Who**'. *Doctor Who YouTube*. 22 December 2013. https://www.youtube.com/watch?v=LWHWQJFSQjo. Accessed 24 September 2017.

'Definition of "Duty of Care"'. *Collins English Dictionary*. https://www.collinsdictionary.com/us/dictionary/english/duty-of-care. Accessed 30 November 2017.

'Do You Think Public Sector Workers Are Paid Better Than Private Sector Workers? Plus, Making the First Move and **Dr Who** Results'. YouGov UK, 17 July 2017. https://yougov.co.uk/opi/surveys/results/#/survey/54be73d0-6ad7-11e7-8cde-a6b53c1dce63/question/a523f700-6ad7-11e7-b4bb-5a4b9f5f534f/toplines. Accessed 10 December 2017.

'Doctor Who: "PS" – Series 7 2012 – BBC One'. *BBC YouTube*, 12 October 2012. https://www.youtube.com/watch?v=XWU6XL9xI4k. Accessed 18 January 2018.

'Jodie Whittaker: **Doctor Who**'s 13th Time Lord to Be a Woman'. BBC, 16 July 2017. http://www.bbc.com/news/entertainment-arts-40624288. Accessed 13 December 2017.

'The Night of the Doctor: A Mini Episode – **Doctor Who**: *The Day of the Doctor* Prequel – BBC'. BBC YouTube. 14 November 2013. https://www.youtube.com/watch?v=-U3jrS-uhuo. Accessed 29 November 2017.

'Russell T Davies: I Wish I Had Cast a Woman as Dr Who'. *Metro News,* 26 September 2017. https://www.metro.news/russell-t-davies-i-wish-i-had-cast-a-woman-as-dr-who/759481/. Accessed 10 December 2017.

Anderson, Kyle, 'Steven Moffat on Clara Becoming the Doctor in **Doctor Who** Series 8'. 15 December 2014. https://nerdist.com/steven-moffat-on-clara-becoming-the-doctor-in-series-8/. Accessed 13 January 2018.

Britt, Ryan, ''Doctor Who' Hating Pears Was a Deep-Cut Easter Egg'. *Inverse*, 27 December 2017. https://www.inverse.com/article/39747-doctor-who-never-eat-pears-easter-egg-paul-cornell-david-tennant. Accessed 10 January 2018.

Brooks, Richard, 'Sexterminate! Doctor Who May Come Back as a Woman'. *The Sunday Times,* 2 June 2013. https://www.thetimes.co.uk/article/sexterminate-doctor-who-may-come-back-as-a-woman-xjzp32mlmj7. Accessed 10 December

2017.

Brown, David G, 'Why *Star Wars: The Force Awakens* is a Social Justice Propaganda Film'. 20 December, 2015. http://www.returnofkings.com/75991/why-star-wars-the-force-awakens-is-a-social-justice-propaganda-film. Accessed 13 January 2018.

Dahlgreen, Will, 'Doctor Who Must Be a Man'. YouGov UK, 4 June 2013. https://yougov.co.uk/news/2013/06/04/doctor-who-must-be-man/. Accessed 10 December 2017.

Daly, Emma, 'Dame Helen Mirren: "A Gay, Black Female Doctor Who Would Be the Best of All"'. *Radio Times*, 3 July 2013. http://www.radiotimes.com/news/2013-07-03/dame-helen-mirren-a-gay-black-female-doctor-who-would-be-the-best-of-all/. Accessed 10 December 2017.

Davies, Caroline and David Smith, 'Dr Who? Big Names Lose Out to Matt Smith'. *The Guardian*, 3 January 2009. https://www.theguardian.com/media/2009/jan/03/doctor-who-matt-smith. Accessed 10 December 2017.

Dowell, Ben, '"Amy Winehouse would be a great Doctor"'. *The Guardian*, 6 July 2008. https://www.theguardian.com/media/2008/jul/07/television.bbc. Accessed 10 December 2017.

Duff, Seamus, 'BBC Face Furious Sexist Backlash After Announcing Jodie Whittaker as First Female Doctor Who'. *The Mirror,* 16 July 2017. http://www.mirror.co.uk/tv/tv-news/doctor-who-jodie-whittaker-reaction-10811248 Accessed 13 January 2018.

Ebert, Roger, 'Great Movie: *Shane*'. Roger Ebert.com, 3 September

2000. https://www.rogerebert.com/reviews/great-movie-shane-1953. Accessed 24 September 2017.

Edwards, Dan, 'Sergio Leone'. *Senses of Cinema*, October 2002. http://sensesofcinema.com/2002/great-directors/leone/#b10. Accessed 15 February 2018.

Franke, Alyssa, Whovian Feminism Tumblr post, 4 August 2013. http://whovianfeminism.tumblr.com/post/57350903796/i-like-that-helen-mirren-has-been-saying-the-next. Accessed 10 December 2017.

Franke, Alyssa, 'Whovian Feminism Reviews *Face the Raven*'. Whovian Feminism Tumblr, 1 December 2015. http://whovianfeminism.tumblr.com/post/134336018362/whovian-feminism-reviews-face-the-raven. Accessed 10 December 2017.

Franke, Alyssa, tweet posted 03:25am GMT, 6 December 2015. https://twitter.com/WhovianFeminism/status/6733425574646210 56. Accessed 24 September 2017.

Fullerton, Huw, 'Jenna Coleman Says a Clara **Doctor Who** Spinoff Is "Best Left in the Imagination"'. *Radio Times*, 13 October 2016. http://www.radiotimes.com/news/2016-10-13/jenna-coleman-says-a-clara-doctor-who-spin-off-is-best-left-in-the-imagination/. Accessed 16 January 2018.

Gaiman, Neil, Tumblr post, 28 July 2017. http://neil-gaiman.tumblr.com/post/163530200511/the-first-mention-that-i-know-of-of-a-time-lord. Accessed 10 December 2017.

Galton, Susanna, '**Broadchurch** Star Olivia Colman Jokes that **Doctor Who** Fans Shouldn't Bet Any Money on Her Taking Over from Matt Smith'. *The Daily Mirror*, 12 July 2013.

http://www.mirror.co.uk/tv/tv-news/doctor-who-olivia-colman-jokes-2048660. Accessed 10 December 2017.

Hashimoto, Mizuho, 'Public ready for a Black Doctor Who'. YouGov UK, 5 April 2016. https://yougov.co.uk/news/2016/04/05/public-ready-black-doctor-who/. Accessed 10 December 2017.

Helmuth, Laura, 'The Next Doctor Should Be a Woman. You Should Care Even if You Don't Watch **Doctor Who**.' *Slate*, 3 June 2013. http://www.slate.com/blogs/xx_factor/2013/06/03/matt_smith_leaving_doctor_who_the_12th_doctor_should_be_a_woman.html. Accessed 10 December 2017.

Holslin, Peter, 'Forget Peter Capaldi: It's Time for a Female on **Dr Who**'. *Rolling Stone*, 6 August 2013. http://www.rollingstone.com/movies/news/forget-peter-capaldi-its-time-for-a-female-dr-who-20130806. Accessed 10 December 2017.

Itzkoff, Dave, 'Peter Capaldi Prepares for His Final Season of **Doctor Who**'. *The New York Times*, 10 April 2017. https://www.nytimes.com/2017/04/10/arts/television/peter-capaldi-prepares-for-his-final-season-of-doctor-who.html. Accessed 15 December 2017.

Jeffery, Morgan, 'Steven Moffat on Casting Peter Capaldi: "The Doctor Was in the Room"'. *Digital Spy*, 5 August 2013. http://www.digitalspy.com/tv/doctor-who/news/a503891/steven-moffat-on-casting-peter-capaldi-the-doctor-was-in-the-room/. Accessed 10 December 2017.

Jeffery, Morgan, 'Steven Moffat on Female **Doctor Who** rumours: "It Didn't Feel Right"'. *Digital Spy*, 5 August 2013.

http://www.digitalspy.com/tv/doctor-who/news/a503989/steven-moffat-on-female-doctor-who-rumours-it-didnt-feel-right/. Accessed 10 December 2017.

Jeffery, Morgan, 'Doctor Who series 9 finale review: *Hell Bent* is emotional and exhilarating but fumbles Clara's exit'. *Digital Spy*, 5 December 2015. http://www.digitalspy.com/tv/doctor-who/review/a776101/doctor-who-series-9-finale-review-hell-bent-is-emotional-and-exhilarating-but-fumbles-claras-exit/. Accessed 30 March 2018.

Kelsh, Sami, 'Doctor Who writer Steven Moffat on Missy, the Rani and Killing Characters'. *Cultbox*, 18 November 2014. http://cultbox.co.uk/features/opinion/doctor-who-writer-steven-moffat-on-missy-the-rani-and-killing-characters. Accessed 10 December 2017.

Kissell, Ted B, 'The Depressing, Disappointing Maleness of Doctor Who's New Time Lord'. *The Atlantic*, 5 August 2013. https://www.theatlantic.com/entertainment/archive/2013/08/the-depressing-disappointing-maleness-of-i-doctor-who-i-s-new-time-lord/278380/. Accessed 10 December 2017.

McGee, Ryan, 'Doctor Who: Peter Capaldi can Stay but Steven Moffat Needs to Go'. *Screener TV*, 5 August, 2013. http://screenertv.com/television/doctor-who-peter-capaldi-can-stay-but-steven-moffat-needs-to-go/. Accessed 10 December 2017.

Mellor, Louisa, 'Doctor Who: Steven Moffat on Series 8, Missy'. *Den of Geek!*, 13 November 2014. http://www.denofgeek.com/us/tv/doctor-who/241275/doctor-who-steven-moffat-on-series-8-missy. Accessed 10 December 2017.

Moffat, Steven, 'Doctor Who Series 9 Episode 12 *Hell Bent*: Green Amendments'. BBC Writers' Room. http://www.bbc.co.uk/writersroom/scripts/doctor-who-series-9. Accessed 12 August 2017.

Mulkern, Patrick, 'Steven Moffat Finally Reveals Why John Hurt Replaced Christopher Eccleston in the Doctor Who 50th Anniversary Special'. *Radio Times*, 23 November 2015. http://www.radiotimes.com/news/2015-11-23/steven-moffat-finally-reveals-why-john-hurt-replaced-christopher-eccleston-in-the-doctor-who-50th-anniversary-special/. Accessed 10 December 2017.

Rankin, tweet posted 1:47pm GMT, 4 August 2013. https://twitter.com/rankinphoto/status/364004638640447489. Accessed 10 December 2017.

Reese, Diana, 'The TARDIS: No Girls Allowed as the Doctor'. *Washington Post*, 5 August 2013. https://www.washingtonpost.com/blogs/she-the-people/wp/2013/08/05/the-tardis-no-girls-allowed-as-doctor-who/. Accessed 10 December 2017.

Robinson, Joanna, 'How Doctor Who Delivered a Righteously Feminist Finale'. Vanity Fair, 6 December 2015. https://www.vanityfair.com/hollywood/2015/12/doctor-who-finale-feminist-clara-tardis. Accessed 30 March 2018.

Ruddick, Graham, '*Sun* and *Mail Online* Under Fire Over Nude Jodie Whittaker Pictures'. *The Guardian*, 17 July 2017. https://www.theguardian.com/tv-and-radio/2017/jul/17/sun-and-mail-online-irresponsible-for-publishing-nude-new-doctor-pictures-jodie-whittaker. Accessed 13 January 2018.

Sims, David, 'The Ongoing Outcry Against the Ghostbusters Remake'. *The Atlantic*, 18 May, 2016. https://www.theatlantic.com/entertainment/archive/2016/05/the-sexist-outcry-against-the-ghostbusters-remake-gets-louder/483270/. Accessed January 13, 2017.

Singh, Anita, 'A Female Doctor Who? Not If Politics Has Anything to Do With It'. *The Telegraph*, 26 May 2014. http://www.telegraph.co.uk/culture/tvandradio/doctor-who/10857320/A-female-Doctor-Who-Not-if-politics-has-anything-to-do-with-it.html. Accessed 10 December 2017.

Westbrook, Caroline, 'Betting Ends on **Dr Who** as Peter Capaldi's Odds Shorten'. *What's On TV*, 3 August 2013. http://www.whatsontv.co.uk/doctor-who/doctor-who-news/betting-ends-on-dr-who-as-peter-capaldis-odds-shorten-101973/. Accessed 10 December 2017.

BIOGRAPHY

Alyssa Franke is the author of *Whovian Feminism*, a blog analysing and discussing **Doctor Who** from a feminist perspective. She is also the co-host of the *This Week in Time Travel* and *In Defense Of* podcasts, and has been a regular guest on a variety of pop culture podcasts. She has written for *Bitch Flicks* and *Bust* about pop culture and feminism. She tweets at @WhovianFeminism and blogs at www.whovianfeminism.tumblr.com.

Coming Soon